Also by Jim Afremow:
The Champion's Mind
The Champion's Comeback

THE YOUNG
CHAMPION'S
MIND

THE YOUNG CHAMPION'S MIND

HOW TO THINK, TRAIN, AND THRIVE LIKE AN ELITE ATHLETE

JIM AFREMOW, PhD

RODALE.

An imprint of Rodale Books
733 Third Avenue
New York, NY 10017
Visit us online at RodaleKids.com.

Copyright © 2018 by Jim Afremow

Rodale Kids books may be purchased for business or promotional use or for special
sales. For information, please e-mail: RodaleKids@Rodale.com.

Printed in the United States of America

Book design by Yeon Kim

Library of Congress Cataloging-in-Publication Data is on file with the publisher.
ISBN 978-1-63565-056-3   hardcover

Distributed to the trade by Macmillan
2   4   6   8   10   9   7   5   3   1   hardcover

If you want to be great, do it.
There's nothing holding you back.
It's all in your control.

—PETE CARROLL

CONTENTS

INTRODUCTION

SIX INCHES FROM TRIUMPH OR DISASTER

Sometimes the biggest problem is in your head. You've got to believe.

—JACK NICKLAUS

D id you know that there is a playing field between your ears? It's about six inches across, bigger than a softball, smaller than a volleyball. How you train and perform on this playing field will determine how you play on an actual field (or court or course). As a young athlete, your brain is developing at a rapid pace. To help you keep up, this book puts you in charge so you can reap the most from what you sow (at practice, on game day, in the classroom).

The aim of the book is to help you create an "internal" coach for you as an athlete. You will learn how champions succeed day after day. We'll tap into their minds so that you can succeed as well. We will explore the champion's mind because in the short term and the long run, the mind determines failure or success. Remember, the body plays the game, but the mind decides the result.

A good example is basketball star Russell Westbrook's record year in 2017, when he averaged a triple-double FOR THE ENTIRE SEASON. This had been done only once before, by Oscar Robertson in 1962, and his record held for 52 years. Many thought the Big O's feat of 41 triple-double games in a season was an unbreakable record. Yet Westbrook did it. What was most amazing is that as Westbrook piled up statistics, his opponents KNEW what he was trying to do, but no one could stop him. Why? His champion's mind.

In contrast, there are the classic failures (often referred to as a choke or a slump or a loss of confidence and/or concentration), such as what happened in the 2016 Masters golf championship. Defending champion Jordan Spieth was winning by a commanding five strokes heading into the back nine on Sunday. However, the generally unflappable Spieth experienced an epic meltdown by bogeying holes 10 and 11, and then quadruple bogeying 12, the shortest hole on the course, by splashing two consecutive shots into Rae's Creek. After finishing in second place, he explained, "I didn't take that deep extra breath" [that he needed on hole 12]. Under pressure, we can all get quick, tight, and make poor decisions. In other words, we ignore or mistrust the champion's mind.

This book is for young athletes (as well as older athletes who are young at heart). You will learn how to peak your performance and avoid mental breakdowns. Chapters One, Two, and Seven are adapted from *The Champion's Mind*, but they have been updated and tailored for teens. The other chapters cover new and exciting topics. How the book is organized is summarized below.

Chapter One explains the importance of developing a winning mind-set to unlock your prowess in sport, school, and life. To master their craft, champions develop and maintain a complete body *and* mind approach. If you want to become the best version of yourself for ongoing success and happiness, you will need to think *gold* and never settle for *silver* or *bronze*.

Chapter Two presents the key mental skills for peak performance, such as goal setting, mental imagery, and self-talk. Most important, a mind-over-matter approach doesn't develop overnight. While these skills can be applied easily to your game-day play, you will follow the same learning process used to develop your physical skills for maximum overall benefits.

Chapter Three introduces readers to the important concept of *antifragility*. The antifragile athlete seeks out, responds to, and becomes stronger with challenges. You, too, can learn from triumph and disaster and be better the next time out. Several vignettes are provided of young athletes confronting various challenges in their games and lives. In doing so, we will see that it is possible for all of us to respond like champions, get on track, and accomplish our big-picture goals.

Chapter Four examines the *zone*, or flow state, that usually happens when people are performing at their peak in their chosen activity. In this state of mind, we stop overthinking and start trusting. This is the state of mind we are all looking for! We will hear from elite athletes about their own zone experiences. The chapter offers specific methods, reminders, and practices that can help us get into the zone and stay there.

Chapter Five shares tips on the topics of sports counseling, social media, sleep science, and sports nutrition. Experts in these key areas are interviewed for their practical advice for young athletes.

Chapter Six offers detailed scripts to guide you through powerful visualizations. The scripts include visualizations for 10 sports, from golf to gymnastics. By following your own scripts (I'll show you how), you should "see," "hear," and "feel" victory before you achieve it in competition.

Chapter Seven puts it all together into a workable plan. Readers will begin by checking their mental state against the *Mental Game Scorecard*. You'll learn how to build preperformance readiness routines, how to avoid the three big mental errors athletes often make at major events or on the day of the big game, and how to develop the ability to have an emotionally balanced life. Control what you can control to get the best out of yourself!

Let's start training your mind. A level playing field is necessary for fair playing conditions, so that, in theory, no team or player has an unfair advantage. That's not true for the playing field between your ears. By training your mind, you can have a real advantage in determining the final score.

CHAPTER ONE

CHAMPION YOUR LIFE

Champions are everywhere,
you just have to train them properly.

—ARTHUR LYDIARD

Like most teens, you probably have posters in your bedroom of your idols, the so-called chosen ones, chosen by you. It's never too early to be your own idol or champion, as all champions start by developing a winning mind-set. Early on, young minds can absolutely learn to think like world-class athletes and then excel in school, sports and, most important, life.

An aspiring teen mind asks, "What separates the top few from the many in any sport?" *Mentality.* The importance of the mental side of athletics was aptly summed up by Olympic swimming megastar Michael Phelps: "I think your mind really controls everything." Phelps was echoing golf luminary Jack Nicklaus: "If there has been one secret to whatever success I've had at golf, it has been preparedness. Both physical and mental."

So setting the mind (mind-set) *training* is key. Physical ability alone rarely results in superior on-field performance. Naturally gifted athletes are not natural at all. They *want* to realize their potential, starting with using their outstanding physical and mental strengths. Their secret is not secretive or attributable to an innate athleticism or to technical skills—they *train* their minds.

Top athletes are often praised, especially in the media, for their unique natural gifts. For example, soccer great Carli Lloyd has a cannon kick, NBA superstar LeBron James explodes on the court, and San Francisco Giants all-world catcher Buster Posey fires up his team at the plate and on defense. You may or may not have similar gifts—time will tell.

Bet on this for sure: behind-the-scenes preparations, mind-set, and work ethic have enhanced the natural abilities of top athletes. Therefore, if you aspire to be a champion, don't be awed by the glitter of their excellence. Instead, know that they spent many thousands of hours in a pool, on a court, or at a track to build up their bodies and shape their minds.

Think about some numbers. Start at 6 years old; 10 years later you're 16. Start at 10; add 10 and you're in college. Even at 14 (15, and onward), whatever you do in the years that pass will certainly shape your life. In short, start *now*.

Just Google, "youngest athletes in sports," and you'll see an 11-year-old girl who qualified for the US Open, a 14-year-old boy playing in the Masters golf tournament, and many others (young soccer players, rugby players, tennis players—almost every sport has youthful prodigies). Martina Hingis became the youngest Grand Slam singles tennis champion when she won the 1997 Australian Open at age 16.

You, too, can take advantage of the years ahead to develop the mental focus and discipline needed to perform in your sport with a champion's mind and body. The mental qualities of confidence, concentration, and composure are crucial for being a champion in everything you undertake, be it in school, sports, or both.

As you grow, your mental abilities need more attention than your physical abilities. Being young, by definition, means having less experience and having more new experiences. It's natural not knowing what to do. To feel emotions, ups and downs, and excitement is all part of growing up. From moment to moment, your mind is susceptible to performance pressures and situational demands. So you cannot trust your athletic performance to chance. You can't just say, *I'm going to do great, and winning will happen.*

Just as you can build physical strength through training, you can also build mental strength through training. Mental dexterity must be practiced and developed in a planned and purposeful manner so that you can elevate yourself to a champion's mind-set in all endeavors.

Champions are also tested. We all experience similar struggles and deal with demanding challenges in our pursuit of excellence, regardless of age, sport, or fitness activity. To be a champion, your true best self becomes key to personal and athletic greatness. You know—we *all* know—that only those performers who strive for the highest goals can reach their highest levels. They might not win, but they will always remember that they *competed.* A champion *makes* greatness happen, despite the odds.

Of course, most of us are not Olympians or professional athletes. But all of us can acquire a champion's mind-set. Any athlete can learn to think like a champion. Everyone can be a peak performer in the game of life by achieving his or her personal best. We can strive to be the best version of ourselves. It is possible for us to stay "cool" whenever adversity strikes. It is also possible to instill mental fortitude and teach a champion's approach.

Part of the process of becoming a champion requires us to learn, grow, and take well-trained, disciplined action to make lasting change in our lives.

Only a small number of people earn athletic scholarships, qualify for the Olympics, or become professional athletes—that's just sports. This truth is hard to acknowledge, but if you do want to give it a shot, then the ball is in your hands. Now the question becomes: Will you run with the ball or will you drop it?

Understand that the difference between a ho-hum performance and a peak performance begins and ends with your state of mind. Most important, all of us *can* learn to think like champions, but *will* we? Adopting a winning mind-set will help you perform at the top of your game and succeed when you most want to succeed. You have hidden inner potential to tap and unleash your inner champion.

A winning mind-set unlocks your athletic aptitude in competition. Champions develop and maintain a complete body *and* mind approach to their performance—the perfect blend of mentality, athleticism, and technique. They make the best of every situation, consistently work hard, and take the extra time needed to realize their aspirations.

Start by giving yourself a report card. As an athlete, compile your own report by taking a hard, critical look at all aspects of your performance. Begin by thinking about the *mentality, athleticism, technique,* and *strategy* that go into your performance. How would you rate yourself in these areas? How would others rate you? Be sure to stay upbeat, because a negative attitude, poor effort, or an unwillingness to improve your conditioning, technique, and strategy will leave you in the bleachers instead of standing on the medal podium.

Champions strive endlessly to reach their best level by improving their mind-set, fitness, mechanics, and game strategy. Look for various ways to test yourself and achieve success, especially exceptional success in diverse areas. For example, Michael Jordan kept winning in high school, won in college, and then won in the NBA. He also kept an internal scorecard. The key was that Jordan didn't just dream of winning an NBA title, he first made sure to win what was in his immediate reach, then kept adding victory to victory.

Even if you are a great natural athlete, you have to tap your talent. Even if you are on a winning team, you have to continue to push onward and believe that you can improve. "There are no shortcuts. If you want to do something special, there's a price to pay," says Tom Thibodeau, head coach of the NBA's Minnesota Timberwolves.

Which level are you committed to reaching—bronze, silver, or gold? Or to use a horse-racing analogy: win, place, or show. But who wants to just place or just show? That's still losing. No matter what your current performance level, never rule out your capacity to become a champion in your sport and in your life. You can *always* do better. You can achieve your true potential. It is possible to make a major impact on your own life by changing your beliefs and expectations about what you can achieve. Attitude is a decision but also a learned behavior, requiring discipline and energy to sustain.

Recently, some softhearted (maybe soft-headed) folks decided that everyone who showed up at a sporting event got a trophy—a so-called participation trophy. Whether a kid sat on the bench, hit a home run, or scored a touchdown, EVERYONE got a trophy! If EVERYONE gets one, NONE are special. Why not just hand out the same donuts when everyone arrives at the ballpark, gym, or stadium? No, you want a REAL donut, with chocolate, sprinkles, cream filling, just like you want a REAL WINNER'S trophy. Anybody can eat a donut, but few can hit homers, dunk a basketball, or run for a touchdown. Anything less than the best is just a sugar-coated donut hole.

Whether you are a student-athlete, playing for fun, or want to become a professional athlete or a serious contender for the Olympics, being the best you can be today will inspire you to work to achieve superior performance and gain a genuine competitive advantage in sports and all aspects of life tomorrow. Striving for the highest level will give you the best shot for personal greatness.

We all want shining moments and success, but we can achieve this only through hard work, intelligently applied.

Recognize that there will never be a better time and place than right now and right here to become a champion in your sport and life. As author H. Jackson Brown Jr. said, "The best preparation for tomorrow is doing your best today." Or to paraphrase Bob Dylan: You are either busy being born or busy dying. You're young, and youth is the best time to get busy achieving your academic and athletic goals. Think *trophy-winning performance*, whether you are studying for exams, going to practice, or playing in a championship game. Why settle for soggy donuts, or—worse—same old, same old donut holes?

THE CHAMPION QUESTION

Your passion and dedication can't be some-time,
part-time, half-time, or spare-time.
It has to be all-time.

—CARLI LLOYD

What will your life look like when you are thinking, feeling, and acting like a champion? This is the key champion question. Take some time right now to imagine that a major performance breakthrough in your game and life has just occurred and that you have become a champion all day, every day.

In your mind's eye, work your way through a regular school weekday, a practice or training session, and a future competition. Draw together as much detail as possible about what it will look like to be handed a trophy because, at that moment, you are the best you. What specific actions or behaviors do you see yourself doing better or differently?

Now that you have reshaped and redefined your game, what do you think others will see? What do you want them to see? What would really surprise your teammates, coaches, or competitors? What do others need to know about you? If you could step outside yourself and examine your new performance, what would you recognize in your new attitude and behaviors?

Identify precisely what you do that is hurting/hindering you most *and then eliminate it*. To perform at a champion's level, you must break any bad habits, such as a tendency to arrive late to practice or going through the motions when you get there. Teens easily get into habits, and sometimes "routines" are needed. Teens are constantly looking for some kind of structure. Remember, we are all champions until we beat ourselves.

Make your new trophy story compelling, full of great deeds and excitement, because doing your best is exciting, while not even trying is just a bummer! You need to see it to achieve it. Each time you do this exercise, your champion's vision becomes clearer and stronger. Your new mental picture will get the performance ball rolling in the right direction.

To go a step further, contrast your personal pride and peace of mind that results from pursuing a champion's approach to life with the future potential pain and regret of knowing in your heart that you settled for less than your best (i.e., a bag of donuts). Will you continue to sacrifice to win or accept participation as satisfaction? Or will you keep putting your best foot forward, especially when you feel as if you're not moving forward? Do not settle for donuts. Do the work, and don't worry about the reward.

My favorite description of excellence in the sports world comes from Anson Dorrance, the legendary University of North Carolina women's soccer coach. He was driving to work early one morning, and as he passed a deserted field, he noticed one of his players off in the distance doing extra training by herself. He kept driving, but he later left a note in her locker: "The vision of a champion is some-one who is bent over, drenched in sweat, at the point of exhaustion when no one else is watching." The young woman, Mia Hamm, became a young superstar and one of the greatest players in soccer history.

This concept of "when no one else is watching" is very important to teens, who too often worry about what others are thinking. Ignore what others say. Ignore what you think they think. Focus on working hard "when no one else is watching"—or when everyone is watching.

There are two forces in your life that will make you a better you—those that push and those that pull. The future pulls, the present pushes. You need both, but understand how each works. Having future goals will pull you on to ever greater success, but wanting to work or train now, in the present, will push you to reach those goals. Think of it as algebra: $E=e$, (Excellence equals effort; don't you wish all algebra was this easy?) The harder you work now, the better your achievements tomorrow.

BELIEVE IN YOUR DREAMS

The secret is to believe in your dreams; in your potential that you can be like your star. Keep searching. Keep believing and don't lose faith in yourself.

—NEYMAR DA SILVA SANTOS JR.

Dream big and have a clear vision of what you will look like while pursuing competitive excellence to inspire greatness. What is your dream goal? What does excellence in your game look like when you are fully dialed in and passionately pursuing your dream, becoming the best you can be in your sport? Make the description vivid and powerful enough to give you that burst of adrenaline when you need it, which comes only from connecting completely with your *heart's desire*—your personal best, of course. Think about the Williams sisters—Venus and Serena. Basically, their dreams and enthusiasm took them to the top of the tennis world. They could have not been given fewer resources when they started playing. They wanted BIG TROPHIES and a lot of them. Guess what they have now? A *lot* of trophies.

ACT LIKE A CHAMPION

Champions behave like champions before
they're champions; they have a winning standard of
performance before they are winners.

—BILL WALSH

There is no yellow brick road to excellence. At any moment, the way forward is harder than the way back (trophies are hard to get, donuts easy). Practice imagining you are a total champion each day and eventually (who can say when?) you'll win. Now is the time that the rubber meets the road (or polyurethane if you're wearing running shoes). You are confident, focused, energized, and in charge. How different it feels to go trophy hunting instead of benchwarming a box of donuts.

Are you arriving early to practice or running late? Are you making weekly plans for training or just winging it because you're too tired or too busy? Are you making the extra effort needed for excellence?

• *Be a scholar athlete.* Get your homework done on time, be prepared for class on time, and go to practice on time.

- *Be a champion at home.* Is your room a mess? Shock your parents by cleaning it up. Does something need to be done around the house? Then get it done.

- *Be a leader.* Is there a school club where you can be a leader? Then lead by volunteering to do more and bring others with you.

According to an Apache proverb, "It's better to have less thunder in the mouth and more lightning in the hand." Actions really do speak louder than words, so take a moment right now to ask yourself, "Am I walking (or running) the walk or just talking about preparing myself for school and sports?"

Some days you will not feel motivated or your nerves are fried. You will feel as though you have only your B- or C- game ready. This moment is a decisive moment. Imagine, for example, that you are experiencing prepractice dread. Resolve to spend the first 30 minutes attacking your workout with enthusiasm, as you really do love it. Most of the time, you will continue in the same manner because you will be rolling along, achieving and feeling better than you did earlier.

The best and quickest solution for overcoming your inner resistance, challenging old patterns, and changing bad habits is to act until you either find your A-game and recover your form—or fail. Strive to be Tom Cruise in *Mission Impossible* or Gal Gadot in *Wonder Woman*. Sure, they're just acting, but they're darn good at acting. Find it, do it, and do it well.

Sometimes, you must do the one thing you don't want to do (e.g., going to the gym or sticking to your nutrition plan). Rather than giving in to your fears and anxiety by clinging to the familiar (e.g., postponing the workout until tomorrow and goofing off with your friends) keep moving forward; it's a nondecision since you *must* do it. Each time you choose to excel, you are making a choice in a forward direction that will determine whether you accomplish your sports goals. Realize that this choice is *your* choice—either *act* like a champion or be a participant.

Here is a bag of sayings on small strips of paper. Take one . . . no, take them all: Stand tall and walk strong. Push right through your impasses. Keep your head in the game. Maximize your mental resources. Eventually you will develop positive ways of being and performing that will become automatic. This strategy is a game changer that will wire your brain and body with peak behaviors and emotions. Acting like a champion really works if you work at it. So, begin working *now*.

MAKE EACH DAY COUNT

It is not hard to be good from time to time.
What is tough is being good every day.

—WILLIE MAYS

If your efforts could be measured in coins (pennies being so-so workouts and quarters being tough-tough workouts), choosing to just show up daily for that participation trophy at the age of 10 and continuing with that attitude to the age of 20 would give you $36.50. In contrast, working harder to win and continuously striving to win from your 10th birthday to your 20th would give you $912.50. The more effort you invest, the bigger the payout.

Excellence can be achieved only *today*, the only day you have to maximize your talents and minimize your distractions. Your challenge is to win in all aspects of life, and to reach that goal, you need to set yourself up for success by *winning one day at a time*. "When you improve a little each day, eventually big things occur," said legend-ary basketball coach John Wooden.

Setting daily goals and striving to achieve them is how you reach the status of a champion. How are you getting better *today*? What will you achieve *today*? Participation trophy holders have a yesterday attitude by dwelling on things that didn't go well in a previous performance or a tomorrow attitude by procrastinating and not getting things done *now*.

Take a "win the day" approach, whether that means getting in extra practice, protecting your rest and recovery time, or crushing it on the field. More math: You usually practice two hours every day. That's 730 hours a year. If you slack off for *just* 10 minutes a day, you'll practice for only 669 hours, spotting your opponents who didn't slack off by about 60 hours a year. Do that for 10 years and you lose 600 hours of practice.

What do you need to do today to put yourself in a more favor-able, positive athletic position? As a champion, you should never settle for less than you can be, but you must also realize that you do not need to be disciplined every second of the day. You only need to be disciplined for those few key moments during the day when you need to avoid temptation and/or start a positive action. For example, does your mind wander during some free moments in class? Or, instead, do you take a few breaths and jot down some thoughts on what you'll do later in practice?

To perform at a champion's level, recognize when it is critical to maintain discipline and when it is time to relax—that is, to clear your mind and enjoy your downtime. What are your main tempta-tions? Does texting get in the way of paying attention to your teacher? Do peers want to goof off when you should be getting ready for practice and warming up?

To begin, what are your most positive actions? Do you surround yourself with positive friends? Do you stick to your routine to stay well rested so that you can give 100 percent in practice?

Recognize that there are some moments during competition that require iron self-discipline, but there are other moments where it is best to take a breather. For example, a golfer must be disciplined when it is time to follow his preshot routine (mind on golf). During the time between shots, however, he can open his focus and relax while he walks down the fairway (mind off golf).

Use the phrase "Think gold" as your mantra for self-discipline during the moments when discipline is absolutely required. For example, consider shouting, "Think gold!" (or "Personal best!") to yourself—or imagine hearing these words booming from a loudspeaker—whenever you have an important choice to make, such as in the morning when you are deciding whether to hit the snooze button and keep sleeping on a cold, wet day or to get out of bed and train for your sport.

YOUR DAILY GOALS CHECK

Success isn't owned. It's leased.
And rent is due every day.

—J. J. WATT

At the start of your day, ask yourself,
"How will I achieve my goals today?"

(INTENTIONS)

At the end of your day, ask yourself,
"How did I achieve my goals today?"

(ACCOUNTABILITY)

THE CHAMPION'S WILL-DO-NOW LIST

You don't have to like it, you just have to do it.

—NAVY SEALS

A common refrain from teens is not having enough time or energy to excel in the classroom, dominate on the field, and social-ize on top of everything else. To perform at a champion's level, you must have a winning off-field game plan that includes specific strategies—for instance, well-placed environmental cues that you can use to achieve excellence and to remind yourself that you are working to win. Tape a note that says, "Think gold," somewhere noticeable or make it the desktop background on your computer to motivate you to start and continue your day with a winning mind-set.

THINK GOLD

Schedule automatic, electronic "think gold" or "personal best" reminders throughout the day; for example, set the reminder func-tion on your cell phone to chime at certain times and display "Champion." If at specific times during the day you feel tired or vulnerable to distractions—time-waster stuff on the Internet or junk food—then schedule your "think gold" electronic reminder for these times.

Stress management is energy management. Stress is a normal and necessary part of life that helps us to meet challenges and overcome them. However, too much stress and insufficient recovery can result in health problems and burnout. Find a balance between alert and explosive energy output and calm relaxed recuperative energy. Think energy output versus idling—how your performance engine functions.

Idling is how you relax and recover from a demanding schedule. Self-care examples include getting a good night's sleep, taking a short nap, attending yoga classes, and eating wisely. These practices will help keep your performance engine working at an optimal level so you can get more geared up, fired up, and focused for school and sport.

Time management is priority management. Prioritizing your time, whether you are a student-athlete or playing with friends, should be an essential part of your daily and weekly game plans. For example, outline your agenda—your pursuit of a championship—each day. Make good choices regarding how you invest your time, energy, and resources. *Champions are on time and on mind for every practice every day.* This allows them to be successful consistently.

Always remember the key word *fun* and include some fun in your daily activities, because a little fun goes a long way in a satisfying and successful life. Whatever activities or hobbies you enjoy, *enjoy* them. In return, you'll get renewed energy from these mental time-outs and achieve excellence. Champions know that no one is going to live their life, do their training, or compete for them. Champions are champions because they take charge of their lives and do what they consider best for themselves.

Schedule the right number of daily challenges. An unrealistic plan is a self-defeating plan. Undoable plans are disheartening, so schedule a reasonable number of tasks. At sunset, savor what you've done—so far.

Daily agendas and to-do lists are excellent tools to help you achieve maximum efficiency and productivity. Challenge yourself to stick to your plans for school, sports, and socializing for the week. But try not to have many fillers or unimportant items on your list. To perform at a champion's level, your to-do list must be a *will-do-now* list.

You are stronger than the initial discomfort experienced in staying disciplined while working hard or changing habits. To achieve positive outcomes, imagine the good feeling of striking off each item on your list. Life is a series of choices, and time is treasure. So, own your game by making good choices and using time wisely.

To enhance your daily performance, put a small gold dot on the back of your hand or wear a gold wristband. These visual triggers are positive reminders for firing up your best attitude, putting forth your full effort, and maintaining a champion's outlook on life. The gold dot or wristband is forever linked to the "think gold" note and goes wherever you go.

Organize to synchronize. Many of us also need to make a commitment to get and stay more organized for greater efficiency and peace of mind. Do you have well thought out meals planned for each day, including balanced snacks? Do you have a packing plan when traveling to compete? Coordinate this with your parents.

A good idea before traveling to a competition or club sport practice is to pack your kit a day early. Lay out your clothes, gear, an extra towel, balanced snacks (raisins, peanuts, and bananas), bottled water, and cash. Then charge your cell phone and iPod.

Keep in mind that other organizational changes in your life can boost your mood and performance. For example, maintain a clean, clutter-free bedroom, desk, and sports locker, use color-coded file folders to sort all paperwork; recycle whatever you can; and keep a daily planner filled only with necessary reminders. This will help you to address distractions, such as playing games on a cell phone, multiplayer games, social media, and peer pressure.

Periodically, spend 30 minutes organizing and cleaning your

space to avoid major disorganization. Less clutter in your personal environment will decrease your stress level. Music can be quite powerful, and we all now have 1,000 songs in our pockets, as Steve Jobs said when he introduced the iPod. This can help us to be champions while organizing and cleaning as it provides a boost in mood. Don't stick with what you always play. Be adventurous: experiment with jazz, classical, hip-hop, classic rock, heavy metal, country, zydeco, and trance/techno music. You might surprise yourself with what music appeals to you in different situations.

WORK ON YOUR PEOPLE SKILLS

Caring about one another and building relationships should be the most important goal, no matter what vocation you are in.

—DEAN SMITH

Social relationships can support and/or put up roadblocks to your pursuit of excellence. As such, people skills can be just as important as athletic ability when it comes down to your enjoyment and success at sports. People skills amount to understanding ourselves and others, talking and listening effectively, and building positive and productive relationships.

The best athletes/leaders are perceptive at reading situations, not just game- or sport-related, but also people, relationship, and feeling situations. Whether you participate in an individual or team sport, good people skills are essential for helping you to relate well and avoid or resolve conflicts with others—coaches, teammates, media, athletic trainers, officials, opponents, family, and friends.

Here are several points about developing good people skills:

Know your rights and entitlements. Do not let others violate these.

Do not tolerate verbal, physical, or sexual abuse. Bullying is not acceptable. You should not be bullied, and you certainly should not bully someone else. When someone's behavior violates your rights, let them know immediately instead of waiting to see if it happens again. Ideally, this should be stated clearly. Likewise, you should respect the rights and entitlements of others by avoiding online shaming, bullying, and trolling.

Be present while listening. Put down your cell phone and give the other person your complete attention, rather than multitasking with a tweet or sending a text. Maintain an attentive posture, make eye contact, and nod in agreement. Summarize what the other person is saying to convey your understanding. Good listening skills encourage conversation. Remember, to listen is to hear, but not necessarily to agree.

Avoid mind reading. Ask the other person what he or she is thinking, feeling, or experiencing rather than telling them what you think they feel. Likewise, others should not have to guess what you are thinking, feeling, or experiencing. Always keep the lines of communication open and respectful.

Discuss problems when they begin. Do not allow a problem with another person to grow into something much bigger. If needed, take a short break (or perhaps even a full day) to clear your head or calm down, and then express how you feel and what you want corrected. This approach can resolve any misunderstanding quickly and get things back on track. Sulking about the issue does no good. Problems rarely go away on their own. They can be frustratingly stubborn. Deal with them now before they become bullies.

Criticize the behavior, not the person. Instead of saying, "You are such a jerk," which will likely be taken personally, a more productive approach would be to say, "When you said that about me in front of the team, I felt insulted. Why did you do that?" It is always better to be specific about the behavior you are challenging. Avoid generalizations such as "You never . . . " or "You always. . . ." Being human, we *never always* do anything.

Let fairness rule the day. Stop trying to be perfect or expecting others to be perfect. Look for a way to compromise when differences arise. In relationships with others, just ask yourself, "What is fair and reasonable to both parties in this situation?" The goal is to work together to find a solution that suits everyone. Avoid thinking in right-wrong, all-or-nothing, or good-bad dichotomies.

BE THE TYPE OF TEAMMATE YOU LIKE PLAYING WITH

What type of teammate do you like playing with?
Be that type of teammate yourself.

—JOHN CALIPARI

The Japanese story "Ten Jugs of Wine" illustrates the difference between being together on a team and *working* together as a team. In the tale, 10 old men decide to celebrate the New Year with a crock of hot sake, a type of Japanese alcohol. Since none of the men has enough for everyone, they each agree to bring one jug of wine for the large heating bowl. On the way to his wine cellar, each old man thinks, "My wine is too valuable to share! No one will know. It'll never show. It'll still be fine. I'll bring a jug of water instead of wine."

And so, when they gathered with the jugs they had each brought, all 10 men poured the contents of their jugs ceremoniously into the big bowl. When it was time to drink, they looked sheepishly at one another: It was plain hot water for all.

Social loafing is a psychological term used to describe the phenomenon of the withholding behaviors demonstrated by the old men in the tale. Specifically, social loafing refers to the tendency of people to try less hard at a task when part of a group than they would when they are alone—responsibility spreads to the group. To be a victorious teammate, however, remember the old men in "Ten Jugs of Wine," and instead do the opposite. Don't hold back, and always bring the absolute best you have to offer from start to finish. Seize opportunities to assist your teammates and to aid the coaches and other staff with anything to help things go smoothly. On or off the court (or the playing field), don't water down your effort by thinking that no one else will notice.

Good T.E.A.M.-mates (Together Everyone Achieves More) help us to become a better player. So always look for ways to bring out the best in one another and depend on your teammates for support as needed. "Building a close team is all about building close relationships—teammates knowing each other and willing to help each other," says Kevin Eastman, former assistant coach and vice president for the NBA's Los Angeles Clippers.

Lauren Murphy is an elite mixed martial artist, a former Invicta FC bantamweight champion and IBJJF Blue Belt middleweight No-Gi World Championship gold medalist. Lauren was awarded the UFC Fight of the Night bonus award for her victory over Kelly Faszholz on February 21, 2016. Even though fighting is an individual sport, I asked Lauren to share how fighters support one another during an elite training camp. She explained:

> A smile and a hello when you walk in at practice goes a long way. Be positive about the warm-up and workout. Shouting, "Let's do this!" gets you jacked up as well as your teammates. Clap, cheer, and make a big deal about what the other fighters are doing right, especially if it's a part of their game plan for an upcoming fight. Praise others when they're doing well, "This is the best you've ever looked," "Your leg kicks are so

3. What are the specific action steps I will take to be a better teammate moving forward (e.g., hustling on every play, being more vocal on the field)?

4. Do I ask questions? (e.g., What can we do differently?)

5. How can I be more respectful and personable? (If any member of your team knows he or she can come to you at any time with a concern or suggestion, it will help create a cohesive team.)

BE A CHAMPION LEADER

Leaders aren't born, they're made. They are made by hard effort, which is the price which all of us must pay to achieve any goal which is worthwhile.

—VINCE LOMBARDI

Skilled leadership is key to developing and maintaining a championship-caliber team. Every member of a team, not just the coaches or the designated captains, can and should be a leader. Everybody should look for opportunities for leadership and think about ways they can positively impact their teams. When all team members embrace this belief, their chances of forming a championship-caliber team increases greatly.

While it's natural for a team or athlete to have a winning attitude when the scoreboard is in their favor or during a winning streak, a champion leader understands that it's during the tough times that a great attitude is most needed. Rather than pointing fingers or complaining in the face of a loss or a lackluster performance, a champion leader has the attitude, "We're all going to get better and find a way to make this work."

Become a champion and a leader of champions. The personal-

hard," "You were fantastic in your sparring rounds," "You opponent doesn't have the team we have," "Your striking looks great," "Your cardio is off the hook," and "Your hard work is paying off."

When you're giving corrections, avoid don'ts such as, "Don't let him get the takedown" or "Don't let him hit you with his right hand." Also, avoid negative comments like, "You need to cut off the cage better." Instead, provide positive instruction, "Step to your left when he steps to his right." If someone had a rough practice, provide encouragement, "You're getting better. You were super-tough and never quit, even though you lost the sparring round. It's okay, it's just practice. It's going to be hard. If it was easy, everybody would do it." So remember that everybody has a bad day. Every single person. If every day is perfect and you're winning every round, you're in the wrong gym.

Championship teams often use terms like *chemistry, togetherness* and *one heartbeat*. Trust is the foundation for the strong "we" feeling on championship teams. Everyone is pushing (or pulling) in the same direction. Keep fighting, stay positive, and do it together as a team to break through poor starts or losing streaks. Always look for a way to help your team tackle the challenge at hand. A team has a shared destiny and, as such, all behaviors must be for the benefit of the team and the greater good.

Think about these five self-reflection questions regarding your role as a teammate:

1. What am I doing that is hurting my team (e.g., complaining, gossiping)?

2. What am I *not* doing that is hurting my team (e.g., cheering for my teammates, accepting my role on the team)?

ity and mentality of any team comes down from the person leading them. We all want to be treated well, so it's critical that leaders model respect and positivity when dealing with others. It is important to be honest and straightforward in your communications with others, but it is just as important to convey your thoughts in an encouraging manner.

TEN ATTRIBUTES OF A CHAMPION LEADER

1. Champion leaders have a successful vision for their team and stay enthusiastic about achieving and maintaining it.

2. Champion leaders always share credit and accept blame. Great leaders believe in inviting feedback from others rather than resenting it.

3. Champion leaders have a strong sense of confidence and optimism about what they are doing and stay calm and in control during moments of crises. All athletes need to know there is hope, and they will look to team leaders as well as coaches for positive cues. So if you're scowling or angry, the team may lose their focus and give up even trying. You don't want your facial expression to result in them feeling like they are disappointing you. For them to maintain hope, they need to know you haven't lost hope in them!

4. Champion leaders take an interest in the person wearing the uniform, not just their athletic performance during a game.

5. Champion leaders respect and appreciate their own role as well as the roles of others. Leading a team is not a solitary endeavor. It takes the time, effort, and commitment of many people. Be vocal, for example, in thanking your parents for their devotion to getting you to practices and games.

6. Champion leaders realize that their impact goes beyond their athletic performance; lead by example, on and off the field.

7. Champion leaders hold everyone, including themselves, accountable for on-field and off-field behavior.

8. Champion leaders learn to adapt to any situation that arises and try to use a style that will achieve the desired outcome. They discern when a situation calls for a pat on the back, and when a friendly but firm reminder would be more effective.

9. Champion leaders share in the team's sacrifices and hardships by never asking others to do what they are unwilling to do.

10. Champion leaders do the right thing, even when it isn't easy or popular.

ROLL WITH CHANGE

The art of life lies in a constant readjustment
to our surroundings.

—KAKUZO OKAKURA

People tend to dislike change—except bus drivers, babies, and vending-machine technicians. Seriously, life is long and there will be major life changes or setbacks. These can represent a loss of routine, comfort, and our role in the family, team, organization, or community. However, adjustments and transitions are things we can master.

We can adjust to change by maintaining a flexible attitude, which is like a free-flowing stream. Now imagine a boulder in the water, stopping the flow: this is a rigid mind-set. Go with the flow by being curious about how you can navigate around (or even profit from) each obstruction instead of being discouraged by it. Major changes encountered by athletes can include:

- Getting cut from tryouts
- Transitioning from junior high to high school
- Losing one's starting position on a team
- An unexpected coaching change
- Dealing with a major injury
- Not being able to continue in competitive sports

Nonsports-related hardships can include:

- Changing schools because of parents relocating or divorcing
- A death in the family or the sudden death of a young friend
- A relationship breakup
- Financial difficulties
- Geographic changes or homesickness
- Academic challenges
- A change in peer relationships

When you get knocked down by disruptive change, get up right away. The answer for a champion is to "play the cards you're dealt with" by proactively dealing with the situation rather than avoiding it and shielding yourself from disappointment. Remember, the more you avoid, the more you will continue to avoid. Instead, when dealing with change, be proactive rather than inactive.

Maximize positive adjustment by doing the right things, such as confiding in people close to you or with a counselor when you feel emotionally down. Appreciate the people around you and ask for their help when needed. Also, kick yourself back into gear when you are lying, hurting others, or being self-destructive.

Finally, be brilliant with the basics—because the fundamentals never change. The basics include:

- Adhering to your regular exercise or training program
- Sticking to your nutrition plan
- Maintaining a regular sleep schedule
- Taking time to relax and unwind
- Feeling what you need to feel
- Spending quality time with others
- Looking for opportunities to help others
- Updating your life goals and avoiding making any rash decisions

Even when you cannot be a starting player in one area of your life because of a major life change or setback, such as an illness, injury, or loss, you can still excel in other areas of your life by tapping into your talents.

FINISH LINE

As we have discussed in this chapter, becoming a champion means that you go for victory—battle against the best *and* be your best—in all areas of your life and game, and not just for those few hours while you're running mile repeats on the track or churning out laps at the pool. The plan is to achieve daily acts of excellence in support of your ultimate dream goal. This is a key concept. Knowing this, ask yourself, "Am I chasing my dreams or just coasting along all day? Am I striving for personal victory (a real trophy) or settling for a participation award?"

CHAPTER TWO

TRAINING YOUR MIND

Learning the mind is as important as knowing the body.
—USAIN BOLT

he science-based mind skills presented in this chapter are proven methods for helping athletes forge a champion's mind-set to reach their peak capability. You will recognize some of these skills, and your challenge will then be to master all of them. You will learn several powerful new skills that you can easily apply to your game play. Adapt each mental skill to fit your needs and situation while pursuing your personal best.

A mind-over-matter approach doesn't develop overnight. Follow the same learning process used to develop your physical skills: repetition (deliberate and daily mental practice) and reinforcement (feeling good about your efforts by saying things like "I'm gaining mental muscle"). To improve proficiency, stick to the improvement plan and try to focus on one or two mind skills many times each day and build a strong, fortified foundation for one of your biggest assets. These mental skills are:

- Enjoyment
- Goal setting

- Mental Imagery
- Self-Talk
- Confidence
- Focus
- Breath Control
- Mental Toughness
- Anxiety Management
- Body Language
- Intensity
- Affirmations

ENJOYMENT

You gotta have fun. Regardless of how you look at it, we're playing a game. I don't think you can do well unless you have fun.

—DEREK JETER

Play is the core of sports. Maybe when you're a professional, the paycheck might be more important than the game, but until then, enjoy playing. Play is what gets a young kid on the court to run until it's dark. Play is what makes a game exciting. Nobody ever cheered people on during an argument in an office.

Running, jumping, pushing, pulling, throwing, and catching— these motions describe all sports. Remember these fundamentals. Enjoy performing them. Don't get paralyzed by analysis or stats. Get out there and run, jump!

Allow time—in fact, put some time aside—to practice and

play in another sport. You don't have to be striving to be the best in that sport; instead, you may just play Wiffle ball with some friends or catch Frisbees with others on a nice afternoon. Moving, eye-hand coordination, and camaraderie are fundamental to all sports, so have a good time playing around with another sport with your friends!

School, sports, and competitions can take you to many places. They can be a great way to travel and see the country and world! If you have the time and resources, take the pre- or post-match time to do a little sightseeing. In fact, you might want to coordinate things the other way around and look for a tournament somewhere that you're interested in seeing. Sport is an activity that transcends language and other cultural barriers and allows people to find common ground.

Whether you're 15 or 50, exercise and staying in shape are important. The modern world is mostly about sitting in a box (a car, a class, or an office) or in front of a box (TV or computer), which is not what the human body was designed to do. We like to move! Finding a sport that you love gives you an opportunity to move around while playing a game, and there's nothing better for your health than movement.

Vitas Gerulaitis, one of the top male tennis players during the late 1970s and early 1980s, was ranked as high as number three in the world in 1978. Despite his ability, Gerulaitis had been beaten by Jimmy Connors a hard-to-swallow 16 times straight. After finally breaking through and defeating Connors in 1980, Gerulaitis declared, "And let that be a lesson to you all. Nobody beats Vitas Gerulaitis seventeen times in a row!"

In reality there is always a winner and loser in every sport. Nobody is going to be on the winning side always, so it's up to you how you approach the days that you lose, because you will lose.

Vitas Gerulaitis had a great attitude. He was in 16 finals of major tennis tournaments and had a great life—nothing to be down about! Sure, take some time after a tough loss, but don't dwell; a loss shouldn't define you.

Along with a positive, enthusiastic attitude, humor and keeping things in perspective are vital to playing sports with a sense of joy over the long haul.

There's great truth in the old saw "humor is the best medicine," or in saying that laughter is "internal jogging." A good sense of humor is important for peak performance, as well as health and happiness. Humor is often misinterpreted in sports as being a sign of distraction or not caring about one's performance. However, finding humor in difficult situations is often the best way to reduce unnecessary stress and increase motivation.

Ultimately, you have to discover what works best for you. Usain Bolt likes to smile and interact with the cameras before he sets up for a race. He has said that this is what works for him, as it keeps him relaxed and helps him to focus. In other words, a touch of humor at the right time keeps things from becoming too tense. A good laugh can reduce stress, boost performance, and improve mood. A coach can lighten the mood and alleviate tension for the team by periodically incorporating fun practice games or activities.

A swim coach, for instance, might surprise the team by having it finish practice with a game of water polo. A baseball team can play a game of kickball, while a soccer team can gather together for a little Wiffle ball. Throwing a football or a Frisbee around can be a lot of fun. At its core, sport about moving around. One doesn't have to be 100 percent in a box all the time. In fact, most people dislike being "boxed in."

What does an umpire say to begin a game of baseball? The

umpire shouts, "Play ball!" not "Work ball!" There is a simple and straightforward reason for this. Sports are meant to be played and enjoyed and enhanced by fun and humor whenever possible.

"Having a sense of humor is huge to me and to our staff because I think if people can't be self-deprecating or laugh at themselves or enjoy a funny situation, they have a hard time giving themselves to the group," said Gregg Popovich, head coach of the NBA San Antonio Spurs.

There is no doubt that this shared laughter can form instant and long-lasting bonds among teammates, as long as stories and jokes are not mean-spirited. Avoid being the person who brings negativity, hate, and anger. Don't belittle others. Here are some practical strategies for enhancing your sense of humor and finding greater enjoyment in your sport:

- Have teammates with whom you share jokes and funny stories.

- Watch humor—comedy movies, TV sitcoms, and stand-up comedians.

- Read humor—comics, funny books, satirical Web sites (e.g., the *Onion*).

- Utilize props—flush away bad performances with a miniature toy toilet that you keep in your locker.

- Be a little silly; everybody likes a clown.

Bottom line: The more enjoyable the experience, the better your performance will be. Baseball manager Joe Maddon guided the Chicago Cubs to World Series victory in 2016, bursting 108 years of pent-up frustration. He said, "Don't permit the pressure to exceed the pleasure." To move forward, seek out things to love about your game and reasons to enjoy it.

GOAL SETTING

I'm very goal oriented. I've always set high goals for myself.
When I was little I never dreamed of going to the Olympics,
but once I did I wanted to do my very best at that level.

—KATIE LEDECKY

What are your smaller, shorter-term goals? What are your bigger, longer-term goals? What is your ultimate dream goal for your sports career and your life? Examples include reaching a personal best, making the varsity team, earning a college athletic scholarship, running a sub-three-hour marathon, and winning an Olympic gold medal. The important thing is that you define your objectives and clarify what it will take to get there.

To turn your goals into reality, you need a plan to achieve these goals. To perform at a champion's level, know what your goals are and always keep them in focus. There are several potential benefits of setting goals. Specifically, goals increase your drive, effort, and will to strive and succeed. Goals can also increase your awareness of performance strengths and areas in need of improvement. They can light the path that will get you to where you want to end up.

Your dream goal as an athlete, whatever it is, will serve as your guiding star. Then you can commit yourself to performing daily acts of excellence with your dream goal in mind. Speed skater Dan Jansen won an Olympic gold medal in the 1000-meter race at the 1994 Lillehammer Winter Olympics, and he set eight world records over the course of his stellar career. He explained the importance of setting your goals high: "I don't think there's any such thing as setting your goals too high. The higher you set your goals, the more you are going to work—if you don't reach them, then it's still okay, just as long as you set them and then give 100 percent of yourself."

How great do you want to be? How much do you want to win? The key is to identify which goals are most important to you and then write them down and display them on your bedroom wall or another location where you can look to them for motivation. Then set your sights on strategically taking your goals one at a time. That is, focus all your energy, effort, and enthusiasm on executing your improvement plan, step by step, day by day, believing that tomorrow you will be better than today.

The results you get are often based on the goals you set, so the goal-setting process is important. Make sure to enlist the assistance of a friend, teammate, coach, or mentor who can serve as an objective observer and provide encouragement. Ask yourself the following five questions to evaluate each performance goal you set, whether the goal is for next week, this season, or your sports career:

- Is my goal specific?
- Is my goal measurable?
- Is my goal positive?
- Is my goal inspiring?
- Is my goal displayed?

The Olympics are based on some very simple principles, but every four years it captivates the world. You can also utilize a three-level goal system to provide motivation and to determine your achievement levels at a training session, during your next competition, or in an upcoming season: 1) bronze, 2) silver, and 3) gold.

In this performance system, the first, bronze, level symbolizes a desired result that would be a good outcome based on a reasonable assessment of past performances and current capabilities. Silver reflects a significant improvement and being very close to the next objective. Finally, a gold is conferred when you've achieved a best time or delivered a major performance breakthrough.

This approach and system provides three levels of success rather than a narrowly defined target goal. There is absolutely no failure in capturing a bronze. Another advantage to this approach is that the top level has no limit, so you cannot sell yourself short by thinking small. At this level, you're pursing the best of the best.

Let's take a look at four creative examples of the three-level goal system in action across different sports:

1. A tennis player with a first-serve percentage of 40 devises with his coach an improvement plan and sets first-serve goals for the upcoming season: bronze: 40 to 44 percent; silver: 45 to 49 percent; gold: 50 percent or higher.

2. A softball player discusses with her coach hitting average expectations for the upcoming season: bronze: .240 to .274; silver: .275 to .299; gold: .300 or higher.

3. A golfer hits 50 percent of fairways. She sets a practice goal to work more on this area of her game. Her goals for the season are bronze: 50 to 54 percent fairways hit; silver: 55 to 59 percent fairways hit; gold: 60 percent or higher fairways hit.

4. A basketball center will work on his free-throw percentages: 60 percent, bronze; 65 percent, silver; and gold by really helping the team out with 70 percent in the bucket.

MENTAL IMAGERY

Visualization is the most powerful thing we have.

—SIR NICK FALDO

Mental imagery, popularly referred to as visualization, is the process of using all your senses to help with learning and developing new sports skills and strategies as well as visualizing success. Imagining your optimal performance is accomplished by creating or re-creating the whole or part of a sporting event. This type of mental rehearsal can be likened to learning a physical skill: the more you practice, the better you will become at the actual task. Thus, imagery goes far beyond daydreaming. As with physical practice, mental practice requires structure and discipline for you to reap the full benefit.

Although imagery will not guarantee that you will always achieve best times or win the game, proficiency in this mental skill will increase your chance of success in sports. Specifically, imagery works to enhance one's performance by sharpening the mental blueprint and strengthening the muscle memory for the physical purpose at hand. This is why imagery is used by virtually all Olympic athletes as a critical part of their training regimens. Imagery can be used to prepare for all athletic performances, regardless of the motor skills involved.

The brain does not always differentiate between real and vividly imagined experiences because the same systems in the brain are deployed for both types of experience. For example, a common nightmare is that of being pursued. The dreamer is safely at home in bed yet awakens frightened—breathing fast, heart pounding. It's all in the mind, yet the dreamer experiences the physical sensations that would accompany a real pursuit. The world we experience exists only in the mind—think about that!

As such, it is worthwhile to visualize positive performances and picture the ideal steps for achieving a successful result. Create a clear mental image and a powerful physical feeling of what you want to accomplish. Include the sights, sounds, smells, tactile impressions, and powerful emotions that accompany the total performance experience while in your virtual arena. The clarity and controllability of your images will improve with practice.

When visualizing, strive to experience the action in 3D from the first-person point of view (through your own eyes), as opposed to a third-person point of view (through the eyes of spectators). This is probably easiest for those of you who have played video games with first-person views of the action. Do the same now in your mind and for your specific sport-related performances. The aim during imagery rehearsal is to "see it, feel it, and enjoy it" (SFE). Experience yourself having achieved your goal through your own eyes, rather than watching yourself from the outside. This will translate into better performances on the field. Here are three key ingredients for successful imagery rehearsal:

1. Vividly *see* what's happening around you while performing successfully.

2. Deeply *feel* yourself performing masterfully.

3. Thoroughly *enjoy* seeing and feeling what's happening while winning.

This type of mind training isn't just for divers on a high platform preparing to dive, or for a sharpshooter aiming at a target. In the NFL, a veteran punter with whom I worked has developed a form of visual weight training for the mind. For 10 minutes every other day, he gets in a relaxed state through deep breathing, and then he "sees and feels" what's happening while executing successful punts in a variety of game situations and weather conditions (using best-, average-, and worst-case scenarios). He uses imagery as a mental walk-through to pre-experience flawless performances and expertly handle any adversity that might occur. He's also familiar with the stadiums on his schedule, so he has visualized himself playing there in his next game. In other words, he mentally goes through something as close to reality as possible. This makes game day more like a routine rather than something unknown.

What images or metaphors do you want to associate with your sports performance? Are they the same as the ones others choose for you? Why did Kobe Bryant like to refer to himself as the Black Mamba? Why did Muhammad Ali like to "float like a butterfly and sting like a bee"? Ali certainly had one of the best sports nick-names ever: "The Greatest." In interviews, Michael Phelps likes to recall how imagining and learning to swim like a dolphin improved his swimming. In fact, images and metaphors allow us to imagine and enter into a high-performance mind-set at levels equal to those in the animal kingdom.

Freestyle wrestler Helen Maroulis said it best: "When I step on the mat, it's like an alter ego. I imagine a jaguar in a cage. That's how I feel when I'm wrestling. I'm really shy off the mat, but on the mat, it's—let's go!" She was the gold medalist at the 2016 Summer Olympics in Rio de Janeiro, Brazil. She beat three-time Olympic champion Saori Yoshida of Japan 4 to 1 in the final match. Maroulis prepares well mentally for her matches and so can you.

Mentally practice two or three times each week for about 10 to 15 minutes per rehearsal (see Chapter 5 for visualization scripts). Select a specific sports skill to further develop or work your way through different scenarios, while incorporating various game-ending situations. Examples include meeting your cross-country race goal time, striking out the side in the bottom of the ninth, or making the game-winning shot just before the final buzzer sounds. In other words, take various expected and unexpected scenarios and put them into your mental reservoir.

A long session is not always necessary, and shorter mental practice sessions are also beneficial. Do you get bored at times throughout the day? Do you fill that gap with a video game on your cell phone? Does that help or hurt your performance?

Good times to go through a brief session include any downtime in your schedule; waiting in line at practice to perform a drill; after practice, to help reinforce what you've learned; or the night before a competition, for mental readiness. This can be as an element of your pregame routine, and especially as part of your preshot routine.

Pull yourself away from some of that social media for a few moments and instead build your own world, mentally walk through a scenario, feel the jitters, and ingrain positive responses in your neural pathways. Go through several scenarios, vary them, look at them from various angles; bring them to life. For example, consider a batter going through swings before his turn at bat. The routine is activating neural pathways and connecting with the moment. Attempt to see and feel making good contact before swinging the bat. This makes it all the more likely that you'll connect with the ball and smack it over the fence!

Let's conclude our discussion with some mental practice. Sit up in a chair with your back straight (rather than lying down on a bed or on the floor, as this can make you sleepy). Close your eyes and become aware of your breathing. Take a few slow, deep breaths (in through the nose and out through the mouth) to clear your mind and relax your body. Select a specific skill in your sport, such as a free throw in basketball or a serve in tennis.

Begin by creating a mental picture of your environment, progressively include all the sights and sounds. Pay attention to the physical sensations in your body, such as the spring in your ankles and knees, whether your breathing is heavy or relaxed, the weight of the racquet or ball in your hand, and the texture of the ball as you spin or bounce it. You may even feel muscles activating in response to your mental imagery.

As you mentally begin your pre-shot or pre-serve routine—for instance, bouncing the ball three times, taking a deep breath, and seeing your target—inhale deeply and let the breath move through your body. Now fully *see, feel,* and *enjoy* executing this skill throughout each moment of the movement. Maintain full attention throughout the activity and complete the routine by sinking the basket with a swish or serving an ace on the line.

Challenge yourself to do this exercise successfully three times in a row with full focus and positive results. If you visualize missing the basket or hitting the ball into the net or if you lose focus, keep repeating the process until you can visualize yourself doing it right straight through. The idea is not to rehearse failures or poor attempts. Instead, you want to go through optimum routines. There is a saying in neurology, "What fires together, wires together." You're wiring your mind and body in successful integrated tightly bound patterns. This will further anchor your physical self to a gold-medal performance.

SELF-TALK

I am a very positive thinker, and I think that is what helps me the most in difficult moments.

—ROGER FEDERER

There is an old Cherokee legend known as the tale of the two wolves. A grandfather explains to his warrior grandson that there are two wolves within each of us: One wolf is positive and beneficial, the other is negative and destructive. The two wolves fight for control over us. The grandson was curious and asked, "Which wolf will win?" The grandfather replied, "The one you feed."

If thoughts determine feelings and feelings affect performance, then thoughts will influence performance. This is a solid-gold truth, so learn to think more positively about yourself and your game. That is, monitor what you tell yourself and always feed the good wolf! This is one of the most important life lessons we learn.

Understand that the choice is yours alone; it is empowering and life-changing.

The first step in feeding the good wolf is learning to identify your own negative and self-defeating thoughts. Typical negative thoughts an athlete can have include "I suck at this," "I'm not good enough," or "I don't belong on the team." We all have these thoughts at times, so take a moment right now to identify some common negative thoughts about your athletic capabilities that run through your mind while you are at practice or in a game. Don't even think about directing such negativity at teammates—don't be a bad wolf!

Now take the second step in feeding the good wolf. Challenge the self-critical thoughts (such as "I'm not cut out for this") with encouraging statements (such as "Bring it on *now!*"). Mentally beating yourself does no good. Instead, gain clear control of your thinking processes. Feed the good wolf and fuel the positive energy. Repeat these two winning steps to build mental muscle, improve your mood, and advance your athletic performance.

When the negative wolf (or Big Bad Wolf) rears its head during competition, stop it right there. Your self-talk (i.e., saying or chanting words or short phrases) should be positive: "I've just made a penalty. I'm getting anxious, I'm dwelling on it. Stop. Breathe. I'm pressing the reset button and deleting that memory from my mind. It's over. I'm going to take a fresh, confident look at the next play in front of me." In quick-reaction sports like basketball and soccer, simply shout to yourself, "Next play!"

In a recent meta-analysis of 32 previously published sports-psychology studies, Antonis Hatzigeorgiadis and his colleagues at the University of Thessaly, in Greece, confirmed that self-talk can produce significant improvements in sports performance. Their article was published in the July 2011 issue of *Perspectives on Psychological Science*. Hatzigeorgiadis says, "The mind guides action. If we succeed in regulating our thoughts, then this will help our behavior."

These researchers also looked at various uses of self-talk for different tasks. For tasks requiring fine motor skills, such as golf, instructional self-talk (e.g., "Do a full shoulder turn" or "Always up, always in") was found to be more effective than motivational self-talk (e.g., "I'm the best"). Conversely, motivational self-talk was found to be more effective for tasks requiring strength or endurance, such as running or cycling.

Self-talk can be more valuable for novel tasks than for well-learned tasks, and both beginning and experienced athletes can benefit from this technique. Although you probably cannot eliminate all negative thoughts, you do have the power to ignore them or challenge these thoughts and replace them with more positive and useful ideas. As we will see later, the goal in the moment of action is to transcend conscious thinking so that you are fully *experiencing* your performance in the moment (i.e., you are in a flow or zone state). Seek to improve the quality of your thoughts and calm your mind. To achieve your personal trophy, always feed your good wolf.

CONFIDENCE

That's all pitching is, is just confidence in your pitches.
If you have intent behind it, more often than not
you'll have success.

—CLAYTON KERSHAW

Sports-psychology studies and anecdotal reports from winning athletes confirm that confidence is crucial for athletic success. Specifically, self-confidence is a strong belief in one's skills, preparation, and abilities. According to legendary tennis player John McEnroe, confidence in tough situations is the mark of a great player. To *be* successful, you must *believe* that you can be successful.

McEnroe's most famous quote was shouted at an umpire: "You cannot be serious!" McEnroe was completely serious at that moment. He knew he was right. However, you must be careful about this kind of confrontation. Players cannot disrespect the officials. The point to make here is passion and conviction, not blasting the officials. You want to have Mac's passion and confidence and to harness any fury to play harder. Play and play hard, and accept that you're just playing. No sporting event has caused a solar eclipse, a tidal wave, a hurricane . . . the earth keeps turning whether you win, lose, or draw.

Where does this confidence come from? True confidence is a hard-earned mind-set. Golf legend Jack Nicklaus built his confidence through proper preparation, particularly for the four major tournaments a year. He won a record 18 professional major championships, but perhaps his greater achievement was 19 second-place finishes and nine third-place finishes. So in an astonishing 46 major tournaments, he was still in the top three and in contention on Sunday. Everyone in front of him checked the leaderboard to see how far away or how close he was to them—point being they were looking for *him*. Many of the players who beat him are now Hall of Famers. They knew they needed their best because Nicklaus was not going to beat himself. Nicklaus said, "You have to be a legend in your own mind before you can be a legend in your own time."

Demonstrated performance and reflecting on previous successes, high points, and proper preparation in terms of quality and quantity are the two primary ways to gain confidence for competition. To paraphrase sprinter Maurice Greene, a one-time world record holder in the 100 meters, train like you are number two (train your talent), but compete like you are number one (trust your talent). Training your talent is always striving to be better. On game day, play confidently by emphasizing your skills and strengths, drawing from past successes and appreciating the encouragement from your coaches and teammates. Emphasize your strengths and your opponents' weaknesses—not vice versa.

To perform at a champion's level, you must understand the importance of a long-term memory for success and a short-term memory (selective amnesia) for failure. Every athlete fails, but champions do not dwell on their failures. Instead, they focus on positive experiences and keep moving confidently forward. Remember to identify similarities between the challenge at the moment and previous situations in which you have excelled or surpassed your expectations. Tell yourself, "I've done this before and I can do it now." Forget unwanted outcomes and focus on your performance.

Complacency (i.e., taking it easy, taking things for granted) is often the number-one culprit when an athlete or team blows a big lead or loses to an "inferior" opponent (who obviously did not see themselves as inferior). Extremely high confidence is never the problem, provided that you are continuously working hard and intelligently in training to become the best athlete you can be and you have an undying will to win during competition: You can hate to lose, but don't be afraid to lose.

Confidence without complacency keeps you on target when you are playing well and winning. Several self-reflection questions are included here based on the pioneering work on the topic of self-efficacy (a specific strength of belief) by Stanford psychologist Albert Bandura, beginning in the mid-1970s. These questions are designed to raise your confidence as you review your accomplishments, recall positive feedback, resolve to mirror and model your athletic heroes, and listen to reminders of your capabilities.

1. What has been the biggest challenge to date that you have overcome in your sport, and how did you overcome it? Examples include bouncing back from a major injury, busting out of a slump, or completing your first marathon or triathlon.

2. Describe your greatest sports performance to date. Spend a few minutes reliving the glory and magic moments from this performance in vivid color. What helped you make it over the top? What were your thoughts and feelings during the game, match, or race?

3. What are three of your signature strengths or attributes as an athlete? Be honest, but don't be modest in answering this question. Examples include work ethic, mental toughness, and focus.

4. What are three compliments you have received from others that made you feel really good about yourself? Examples include a coach describing you as the hardest worker on the team, opponents saying you were their toughest competition, or a teammate calling you a warrior on the field.

5. Who in your life wouldn't be surprised to see you overcome the challenge before you now and/or accomplish your biggest goal? Examples include your mother, father, sibling, grandparent, coach, teammate, or friend.

6. What are three awards or accomplishments that you have earned? Examples include an individual or team trophy, an athletic scholarship, or a personal best in your performance.

7. Identify three athletic heroes or role models (currently or from childhood) that you can mirror or mimic when you need a confidence boost during a challenging situation. Perhaps your favorite player battled through on-the-field adversity by showing tremendous resolve when he or she played. Remember, if you can see greatness in others, then you already have some of that greatness in yourself.

FOCUS

The idea is to shut out every possible distraction,
and think about your teammates,
so you don't think about yourself.

—STEPHEN CURRY

Focus, or selective attention, is your dedication to the task at hand to the exclusion of all else. In sports, focus requires screening out useless information (fog) to concentrate on the target, such as the bull's-eye in archery or the flag in golf. The preferred sequence is to lock on the immediate target, disregard distractions, and prevail.

Michael Phelps, the most decorated Olympian, with 28 total medals (including 23 golds!), put on his headphones when he went to the pool to get into his own little world. The only thing that mattered to him was swimming his best. Phelps was able to reach a level of focus and drive never seen before in his sport. He discussed the significance of focus in his book *No Limits: The Will to Succeed*:

> When I'm focused, there is not one single thing, person, anything that can stand in my way of my doing something. There is not. If I want something bad enough, I feel I'm gonna get there.

Let's say, for each moment, an athlete has $100 worth of focus and he or she can spend it in any manner. A dollar spent on an internal and/or external distraction during a performance is a dollar wasted because the player is not getting the full value from his or her abilities.

Where is your focus when you compete? Are you caught up with distractions or do you stay on target? Spend all of your focus dollars efficiently on the process of performance instead of any potential distractions. For instance, a goalie in soccer should fully focus on playing moment to moment by tracking the ball instead of dwelling on having just allowed a goal and glancing at the bleachers or at the other team's bench to gauge reactions. Focus keeps external and internal distractions at bay.

COMMON EXTERNAL DISTRACTIONS	COMMON INTERNAL DISTRACTIONS
• Crowd noise • Photo flashes • Public announcements • Scoreboards • Shadows • Trash talk by opponents • Inclement weather (hot/cold, wind/rain)	• Hunger • Thirst • Fatigue • Soreness • Off-topic thoughts • Negative emotions • Boredom

An important realization is that something is a distraction only if you consider it a distraction. Simply look away. Ignore noises (even from your Big Bad Wolf). Focus on your breathing and your body. Be aware of your easing grip on the golf club, hockey stick, baseball/softball bat, or tennis racquet. In sum, trust your five senses to "feel the now" and stay in the moment. That is, always strive to be in the now.

Your thought process must be simplified and concerned only with what is happening now to win or reach your peak performance in sports. Always stay fully focused in the moment on the field of play. Thoughts about the past and future are fog, and thoughts about the present—the here and now—are clear skies. Play with bright blue skies in the front of you and eliminate any dreary, bleary-eyed haze.

Being present in the moment empowers you to respond with alertness, curiosity, and skill to whatever comes your way. Nothing else matters, as your focus is on putting your purpose in the crosshairs and taking your best shot. When you are clearly focused on the present task, then you free yourself to thoroughly enjoy the experience.

Full presence produces seamless fusion—you become your performance (the zone). Otherwise, you are always one step behind what you are doing because you are judging what is happening and are not fully in the moment. A mind in the moment is not self-conscious or concerned about what opponents or spectators are thinking or doing.

Chris Sharma, one of the world's best rock climbers, says he gets so focused when he climbs hard routes that he *completely* loses himself. He channels all his energy directly into what he is doing in the moment of the climb. In the same way, stay within yourself and get *into* your performance and exert your will. It's your day and your chance.

It is natural for your mind to occasionally drift or fog up, but you can decide to focus on the moment's challenges. Keep reminding yourself to "Be all here!" or shout, "Now!" when you discover that your mind has wandered back to the past or forward to the future. Extraneous thoughts should be nipped in the bud.

Through increased self-awareness and mental discipline, you can train your mind to remain squarely in the present. The present is always present (time now), and time past and time future exist only in your imagination.

BREATH CONTROL

Breathe and believe.

—ANONYMOUS

To perform at a champion's level, breathe deeply and rhythmically to maintain peak energy levels. Proper breathing works in tandem with being a Now-ist (i.e., living fully in the moment). Expand your lungs during inhalation and relax them during exhalation. Let your shoulders drop and jaw relax as you exhale.

Give it a try right now. Inhale a deep breath and let it out slowly. Your breathing can become shallow or stop when you feel angry or anxious. When this occurs, oxygen intake diminishes and muscle tension increases. So make sure to take a deep breath in tough situations. The act of prolonging exhalation, regardless of inhalation length, promotes the relaxation response. Proper breathing helps expel stress and tension and brings you back into the present. When you've done this enough times, you'll find yourself taking a deep breath automatically when the unexpected comes up. That's what you want!

Chicago Cubs relief pitcher Carl Edwards Jr. found deep breathing very effective during the 2016 World Series:

> They say that breathing slows the game down. So for me, when I'm pitching, I'm always taking a deep breath. When I do that I feel like it strengthens up my focus . . . I feel that's one of the big key elements, especially, like you say, young guy in the World Series, your team hasn't won in so many years, everything on your shoulders right now. What you gon' do? I say breathe.

Check on your breathing throughout the day. Are you breathing from the belly or from the chest? Is your breath deep or shallow? There are three simple steps to taking a deep, centering breath:

1. Breathe in through your nose on the count of one, two, three, four, and five.

2. Hold for one and two.

3. Breathe out through your mouth for a count of one, two, three, four, five, six, seven, and eight.

Mentally count to five for the in breath, count to two as you hold the breath, and count to eight for the out breath. Take your time with this 15-second breathing intervention and repeat the steps for four cycles (your one-minute breath workout) or as many times as desired. Do this exercise when you feel that you are getting tense, feel down, or feel stuck in a repetitive negative thinking cycle. Breathing in this manner will help you to slow your heart rate, calm your thoughts, and find inner stillness in the moment.

Learn how to sit quietly without doing anything other than listening to your breath. This is helpful because it feels more active. Listening to your breath works well for those who are often distracted or feel the need to do something. Extraneous thoughts fog your focus. Your mind becomes more powerful as it becomes calmer and clearer. So breathe deeply and mindfully throughout your day. Also, when you are not thinking about the future, it's difficult to fear it. Fear is the enemy of effective action!

MENTAL TOUGHNESS

The measure of who we are is how we react to something that doesn't go our way.

—GREGG POPOVICH

Being tough in your mind does not entail clenching your teeth, thinking more, straining your eyes to focus, risking a serious injury, or steeling yourself when someone screams, "Be tough!" at you. Mental toughness is the ability to remain positive and proactive in the most challenging of circumstances.

A tough mind is built on doing hard tasks over and over again, especially when you don't feel like doing them. Push through on your down days when you are not feeling your best. Distractions, discomforts, and difficulties are no match for the mind of a champion.

This dogged determination requires moving forward through inconveniences, substantial discomfort, and insecurities to reach your top goal. When you want something really badly, don't give up until you've got it.

Having that sort of mental toughness can be demonstrated at a particular moment in time or over the long term, as in your overall career success. Doing a task that is hard over and over again is like depositing money in your inner-strength bank account.

Distance runner Emil Zatopek is one example of an athlete who used mental toughness in his training to reach the top. He won three gold medals in the 1952 Helsinki Olympics, including victory in the first marathon he ever entered. Overall, Zatopek won a total of five Olympic medals: four golds and one silver.

Dubbed the "Czech Locomotive," Zatopek said, "If one can stick to the training throughout the many long years, then willpower is no longer a problem. It's raining? That doesn't matter. I am tired? That's beside the point. It's simply that I just have to."

Around the time Zatopek was tearing up the track, Billy Mills was living in poverty in Pine Ridge, South Dakota. He was orphaned at the age of 12 and was raised on an Indian reservation rife with alcoholism. He turned to athletics for a positive outlet and eventually took up running.

Mills made the US Olympic track-and-field team for the 1964 Tokyo Olympics. He was an afterthought in the 10,000-meter race—his qualifying time was almost a full minute slower than the favorites. To all observers, he was just filling a lane, but Mills decided to win, no matter what. With his fierce resiliency, Mills overcame his lack of international experience, a wicked shove and elbow on the last lap by the world-famous favorite Ron Clarke, and being boxed in on the final turn. In a move only he knew, only he could make, he blasted down the final stretch and won the gold in record time.

Adversity can either beat you or make you tough to beat. Mills's strong mind made him a champion. This is a vastly underrated tale. One of the great Olympic stories.

In the 2007 NFL divisional playoff game between the Green Bay Packers and Seattle Seahawks, Packers running back Ryan Grant fumbled twice in the first four minutes and his team fell behind 14 to 0. He told himself, "It happened, that sucks, gotta move on." This is the crossroads: quit or persevere.

A champion knows that thoughts cause feelings, and feelings affect performance. Rather than retreating into a shell, Grant gave himself a pep talk and ultimately gained 201 yards and scored three touchdowns to help his team to an impressive come-from-behind 42–20 victory. He was able to "fumble and forget" so he could get back to winning.

Grant won the mental game by not letting this situation disrupt his mind-set. He could have said, "Woe is me, and here we go again," but chose to put up a performance that made the fumbles irrelevant.

It is always better to acknowledge and accept whatever happens. Then let it go and focus forward with complete confidence. Grant's attitude was that he needed to keep his head in the game because there was a lot of football left to be played. Always remember, in training or in competition, tough times require tough mental responses. Stay in the game until the clock clicks down to zero.

ANXIETY MANAGEMENT

I'm always nervous. If I wasn't nervous, it would be weird. I
get the same feeling at all the big races. It's part of the
routine, and I accept it. It means I'm there and I'm ready.

—ALLYSON FELIX

Most athletes feel anxious before and during competition.
They accept performance anxiety as perfectly normal and let it
sharpen their focus. This anxiety or excitement is proof that they—
and you—care about performance and outcomes. Of course, too
much anxiety is uncomfortable and interferes with performance.
The key is to strike the right balance and to shift anxiety into a
keener focus.

A moderate level of anxiety or excitement is necessary for optimal performance (write that down and display it wherever you can
read it every day).

Unlike a threatening situation or danger, panic in sports is
typically an extreme form of performance anxiety. A panic
response is thus an exaggerated mind-body reaction—a false
alarm—that must be diffused or redirected.

Our instinctive responses to panic are often counterproduc-
tive, such as fleeing, isolating ourselves, trying too hard to relax, or
beating ourselves up mentally. If you have a high level of performance anxiety, then you've learned a sequence of responses that
aren't helpful to you in a sports situation. Once you trigger the
sequence, it is difficult to stop the dominoes from falling. Your priority, then, is to stop the sequence early.

The most likely trigger is *embarrassment* that you will fail to perform in the moment. However, if you've gone through positive
practices and have a champion's outlook on your sport and life,

what can you possibly be embarrassed about? Remember that panic is a feeling and experience that exists only in your mind and, by extension, in your body. Panicking is not going crazy, but rather the manifestation of fear of a terrible outcome that leads to anxiety and a debilitating loop of panic.

Several tactics can help you triumph over performance anxiety so that you can fully enjoy sports and perform at your best. These tactics are not designed to eliminate intense feelings but to redirect them toward a positive outcome.

Be well prepared. The more prepared you are for competition, the less you will fear it. Nothing helps build confidence more than knowing that you are ready for the challenge at hand. Proper preparation comes from paying close attention to feedback from coaches, studying the playbook or game film, and practicing conscientiously.

Without this kind of preparation, performance anxiety is more likely to occur. Before the game, always remind yourself that you have honestly prepared as best you can. *Nerves are natural.* It's normal to be anxious, so don't concern yourself with what other athletes might be thinking or how well they seem to be doing. Often, we don't suspect that others are overcome or underwhelmed by anxiety. No matter how calm your opponents may appear, they are likely experiencing the same level of anxiety—or more so—than you are.

There's a reason why New England Patriots quarterback Tom Brady is always so calm and positive in press conferences. He's actually putting the fear into his opponents. He's saying he's unflappable and that opponents had better come ready to play.

Ally with the anxiety. Do not attempt to rid yourself of the anxiety; instead, channel it into performing well, and talk to yourself about trying to use your "energy" instead of trying to avoid it. Tell yourself, "My body is preparing itself to perform" and "I've done well before, and I can do it again now." Past performance is past. Now is now, in the moment.

One approach that may help translate this mental energy into a positive physical response is to warm up and then really turn it up for a few quick sprints or other high-intensity movements. The speed will slightly tax your body and tell it that it's ready (go-time). You'll find that your overall system actually calms after this brief intense warm-up.

Breathe evenly and deeply. Take a series of deep breaths to calm your nerves. Good breathing reduces anxiety by clearing your mind of fog and by reducing physical tension. Simply prolonging exhalation, regardless of inhalation length, promotes the relaxation response, so regulate each breath with a deep inhalation and a full exhalation.

Watch closely, as there's a good reason most athletes go through a set routine, for example prior to batting or before hitting a serve. Most likely, they've integrated into that routine several actions, such as taking two or three good breaths and exhales, before moving to the plate or prior to the ball toss. In practice, this was done over and over to become automatic, which is then triggered by the routine in the competition. Practice with intention leads to a champion's performance.

Get creative and use your imagination. For instance, give the anxious feeling an imaginary form, such as a sparkler or firecracker, and then place it in an imaginary safe place or container that will protect you from it. Understand that you are bigger and more powerful than this anxious feeling.

Stay in the here and now. Monitor negative "futurizing" and worrisome thoughts about winning or losing. The results and outcomes can wait while you remain focused on playing each play to the best of your ability, one by one, until the final whistle.

Stay on a positive thought channel. Flip the switch from negative to positive self-talk when you are emotionally spiraling down. Try to talk sense to yourself (feed the good wolf) instead of letting your fear run wild (feeding the bad wolf). Remind yourself, "Even though I am feeling anxious and uncomfortable right now, I can still play well and reach my goals."

Take yourself lightly. A competition is an opportunity to test your fitness, challenge your competitor(s), and demonstrate how hard you've worked. Take what you are doing seriously, but learn to take yourself lightly. Always remember that sport is what you do and not who you are. Smile. Laugh. Have a good time. Ask yourself, "What's the worst thing that can happen?" If the worst does happen, ask, "What can I do to cope?"

To move forward rather than becoming overwhelmed and backing up when anxiety strikes, make use of the strategies presented here to channel anxiety into a commitment to taking the next step. Remember that FEAR means to "Face Everything And Respond." To perform at a champion's level, let the butterflies fly in formation!

BODY LANGUAGE

We put a huge premium on body language, and if your body language is bad, you will never get in the game. Ever. I don't care how good you are.

—GENO AURIEMMA

Body language is nonverbal communication through postures, gestures, facial expressions, and eye movements. Body language is a two-way process: Your own body language reveals your thoughts and feelings to others, and other people's body language reveals their thoughts and feelings to you. The body language of athletes and coaches is easy to pick up on while watching a sporting event, and it is usually representative of who is winning or losing at the moment.

During practice or on game day, what is your body language saying? What image do you want to project? Top athletes project confidence, energy, and coolness in tough situations.

Are you feeling intimidated before playing a top-ranked opponent and does your body language show it?

Positive postures can generate powerful responses. In other words, looking like a winner can help you perform like a winner.

BODY LANGUAGE CAN BE POSITIVE OR NEGATIVE

POSITIVE BODY LANGUAGE	NEGATIVE BODY LANGUAGE
• Smiling	• Frowning
• Chin up	• Shaking your head
• Shoulders back/chest out	• Eyes downcast
• Standing tall	• Shoulders hunched
• Walking strong	• Slouching
	• Dragging your feet

Adopt the pose of a supremely confident athlete for the duration of your practices and games. Acting this way will help you stay in a winning frame of mind, regardless of the score or situation. When you are gassed at practice, stand tall and walk strong. When you are playing an undefeated team, show your swagger. Make eye contact when your teammates or coaches are speaking to let them know you are listening.

Are you prone to making sour facial expressions or showing negative body language after missing a shot on goal or making an error in the field? To perform at a champion's level (and to be a good teammate), keep a positive demeanor and attitude rather than pouting or moping. Your body language will send the right message to the opposition: You can't be mentally beaten or fazed—no matter what happens.

Just smile and you'll feel better. Imagine that one day you are feeling down—perhaps something did not go as well as expected. But there isn't time to figure out things because you must start mentally preparing for that night's game. How can you quickly get into a better mood? Perhaps you've heard the expression "Just smile and you'll feel better." Does the act of smiling itself really make you feel better? Yes, it does.

Findings from a 1988 research study by psychologist Fritz Strack and his colleagues revealed that simply creating a smile by clenching a pen lightly between the teeth will almost immediately make people feel happier about what they are doing. So, keep this in mind when you need a quick boost in mood. Do not simply drag a down mood into your performance. Put a confident smile on your face instead!

Always give your BEST. Psychologist John Clabby has coined a handy acronym for giving one's BEST—"Body language, Eye contact, Speech, and Tone of voice." Strive to always give your absolute BEST: body language (strong), eye contact (focused), speech (assertive), and tone of voice (self-assured). Strive to sharpen these four aspects of your communication further. Working on them at practices will make them automatic in competition.

Dress for success. As a final point, don't overlook your appearance. Wear your uniform with pride. To look cool or aloof, teens often imitate not-so-admirable idols, sometimes even posing like them. Others like a positive person, so don't be Mr. or Ms. Downer.

All sports and competitions are a combination of chance, practice, skill, and competitiveness. While not all of these components are in your control, each performance can be elevated by a strong mental attitude. Techniques to build your mental strength in practices and games include using the BEST routine, valuing your appearance, and putting on a smile to push past your perceived physical limitations.

INTENSITY

Success is much more of a relaxed intensity
rather than an intense intensity.

—JEFFERY COMBS

When athletes are "flowing" or "in the zone," they are maintaining a certain intensity level while being mindful of the moment, which helps them achieve their peak performance. Since a direct relationship exists between performance quality and intensity level, your performance may be poorer when your intensity level is too low (you feel tired or disinterested) or too high (you feel wired or overexcited). For example, if your intensity level is low when competing against an unranked opponent, your play might be sloppy. Conversely, if your intensity level is high when competing against the top-ranked opponent, you may play at too hurried a pace.

Each athlete has an optimal intensity level for peak performance, depending on the sport. For example, golf is a game of calm, serenity, and narrow focus, with controlled explosive bursts. American football, on the other hand, is associated with constant physical contact, running, scrimmaging, passion, emotion, and excitement. While a golfer might need to increase his or her intensity level to blast a long drive, a quarterback might need to be in a zone of tranquility for precision passing as tacklers converge around him.

To find your optimal intensity zone, so that you can perform at your best, you must learn how to power up or power down to the ideal intensity for each situation. For example, a basketball player needs to have intense speed on defense, then quickly shift gears for a controlled run down the court, which ends with a pivot and fade away for a relaxed jump shot. In other words, your intensity must adjust. There are several techniques and strategies to increase or decrease your intensity levels to meet the demands of the game play at hand.

Power up. Imagine that you need to increase your intensity to run sprints in practice or push through your final set of bench presses at the gym. Here are some strategies for powering up:

• Take three to five quick, forceful breaths.

• Picture a powerful image, such as a cannon blast, a warrior gearing up for battle, an erupting volcano, a majestic lion stalking prey, or turbulent winds circling in a tornado.

• Perform dynamic movements, such as stretching out your arms in a barrel hug, squat low to burn your thighs, or clap to a slow, thundering, rhythmic beat.

• Repeat energizing thoughts, such as "I am strong!" or "Get it on!" or "I will conquer this!"

• Replay in your mind a favorite upbeat or high-energy song, one that always gives you a rush. Sing or hum it to yourself.

Power down. Perhaps you need to decrease your intensity level at different points in a game, such as between periods of a hockey game or innings of a baseball or softball game, or as you employ different tactics. This can conserve your energy and improve your focus for the next period or inning. Here are a few ways you can dim the lights:

- Take three to five deep, calming breaths, with each being slower than the last.

- Imagine a serene scene, such as a still lake nestled among mountains or a breeze rippling through a field of tall grass.

- Perform light stretches.

- Think calming meditations, such as "Clear mind, relaxed body."

- Replay in your mind a favorite mellow song. Sing or hum it to yourself.

Most athletes are in an underactive mode during practice sessions ("I've got better things to do"), which dampens their intensity and may cause them to play sluggishly, and an overactive mode during games ("I cannot lose this game!"), which increases their anxiety and may cause them to play erratically.

The next time you are practicing or competing, ask yourself, "Is my intensity level too low, too high, or just right?" Adjust it accordingly to respond optimally to the situation at hand. As a leader, motivate teammates who slack off in practice by raising your own intensity, which raises your teammates' performance.

Practice at your optimal intensity, learn to shift intensities, and create an ability to draw upon the right intensity during a match. In other words, if you figure out what your optimal intensity would be during a match and play with that intensity during practice, it will be easier to get into that intensity zone during the match. Playing within your optimal intensity zone, like any other crucial athletic skill, takes practice before you can successfully carry it over in a match.

AFFIRMATIONS

We want our players to say, "This is who I am, this is how I'm going to play, I've got the discipline to do it."

—NICK SABAN

Attitude is the key for peak performance. Develop a list of affirmations to ignite your inner champion. Make sure each statement is meaningful so it really speaks to you. Then write your statements down on your iPhone's note function or on an index card and read them for an extra mental boost. NBA superstar Kevin Durant writes "Have Fun" or "Smile" or something similar on his game shoes to remind him *why* he plays basketball (fun) so that he doesn't become too tense on the court. The more you repeat your power phrases with meaning and conviction, the more real they will become in your mind and the sooner they will enable you to manifest change in your life.

> As a single footstep will not make a path on the earth, so a single thought will not make a pathway in the mind. To make a deep physical path, we walk again and again. To make a deep mental path, we must think over and over the kind of thoughts we wish to dominate our lives.
>
> —*Henry David Thoreau, author and philosopher*

> I think it's very important to have a feedback loop, where you're constantly thinking about what you've done and how you could be doing it better. I think that's the single best piece of advice: constantly think about how you could be doing things better and questioning yourself.
>
> —*Elon Musk, entrepreneur (Tesla, SpaceX, PayPal)*

Be mindful and build your positive talk.

Keep to the present tense in creating personal affirmations. For example, say, "I am" rather than using the future tense, "I will become." Why? Because we always live and perform in present time, not in the future. The subconscious does not recognize the future; it understands only the here and now. Here are some power phrases that you can repeat to elevate your performance to a champion's level:

- I smile and have fun
- I trust my talent
- I make the next play legendary
- I run first in practice and games
- I play for stories of glories
- I have an attitude of gratitude
- I encourage and support my teammates
- I stay in the present
- I commit to the process
- I am grateful for the opportunity to compete
- I perform to a positive self-image

FINISH LINE

To earn your personal trophy, you must possess and cultivate a champion's mind-set. The aim of this chapter is to provide you with an increased understanding of how the mind is important to your game. You now have at your disposal the mind skills—such as mental imagery, confidence, and focus—for creating a champion's mind-set to achieve consistently higher levels of personal performance.

Follow the exercises and recommendations provided to build a rock-solid foundation for your mind and approach to your game. The result will be better on-the-field and off-the-field performance. Be positive and strong in mind and body.

CHAPTER THREE

THE ANTIFRAGILE ATHLETE

**No matter what happens, it is within my power
to turn it to my advantage.**

—EPICTETUS

our ultimate goal—to be the best, strongest, and smartest version of yourself for long-term success and happiness—is always possible . . . *if you pursue what is most important to you.* To succeed (win), make your life as antifragile as possible. Antifragile is a term coined by Nassim Taleb in his wonderful book titled the same.

According to Taleb, you can follow three pathways in life: 1) fragility, 2) robustness, or 3) antifragility. Basically, these three terms refer to how people respond to various stresses, such as volatility, randomness, pressure, discomfort, mistakes, losses, turmoil, and so on.

• **Fragility:** Something that is fragile reacts *negatively* under pressure. For example, consider glass or ceramics that break when dropped. These items must be packaged in bubble wrap and shipped with labels indicating "Fragile" and "Handle with Care" to prevent damage. Similarly, an athlete who is fragile will get knocked backward or down when facing an adversary.

• **Robustness:** Something robust or resilient responds *neutrally* to stress. For example, solid materials like steel or stone resist breaking and are likely to pass easily through the mail. Similarly, a robust athlete withstands stress and doesn't tilt toward better or worse.

• **Antifragility:** Something antifragile responds *positively* to disorder, turmoil, error, chaos, and bad luck. Antifragile is thus the opposite of fragile. Muscles can be antifragile. For example, the stress and discomfort of strength and conditioning exercises elicits a response from your muscle that make them stronger in response to the stress. In a similar way, an antifragile athlete seeks out, responds to, and become stronger with challenges. Champions learn from triumph and disaster and are better the next time out.

Looking at the pros, Aaron Rodgers—Green Bay Packers quarterback, Super Bowl champion, and two-time MVP—is the personification of antifragility. He's dealt with naysayers, injuries, losses, mistakes, rivalries, and tough competition to reach the top. Here's Rodgers explaining his antifragile attitude on the *Stephen A. Smith Show*:

> When you embrace the challenge every single year of a different team, injuries, adversity, the ups and downs of a season, that's why we play the game. That's the exciting part and I look forward to those challenges every single year because it's a mystery.
>
> You don't know what the team's going to be like, how it's going to shake out, how the leadership is going

to rise up from certain guys at different positions, how guys are going to grow, what guys might stumble a little bit. You've got to pick up and get on the way with your guys. Injuries obviously play a big part in that. I look forward to that.

Rogers has described for us how the best athletes have often failed the most, but they always fall *forward* rather than being knocked *backward*. In a similar way, poet Kahlil Gibran argued, "Out of suffering have emerged the strongest souls; the most massive characters are seared with scars."

Let's use Major League Baseball as an illustration. Who is the all-time leader in losses for a pitcher? Cy Young. Who has given up the most walks? Nolan Ryan. Who has been caught stealing the most? Rickey Henderson. Who has the most strikeouts as a hitter? Reggie Jackson. What do all of these players have in common? **The Baseball Hall of Fame!**

If there were no stressors or challenges in your life, you would not step up your game because there would be no need. In fact, our bodies do not do well with a complete absence of stress. Astronauts living and working in space begin to physically deteriorate without the force of gravity they experience on Earth. Rather than being too comfortable, we need our own "gravity." As a student-athlete, tough classes are good for you. Hard training is good for you. Difficult competition is good for you. Constructive criticism is necessary.

Know that you will become better through your struggles. As musician and writer Henry Rollins said, "Scar tissue is stronger than regular tissue. Realize the strength, move on." Crave challenges and embrace your stressors. Be proud of your "scars" from the hard lessons learned rather than ashamed of your failures.

Every team should strive to be an antifragile team. As Ohio

State football coach Urban Meyer argued, "Every team faces adversity. Mediocre teams are destroyed by it. Good teams survive it. Great teams get better because of it." How will your team respond to a demanding schedule, tough opponent, and devastating loss? You can lead the way with great leadership by demonstrating an antifragile attitude.

Bear in mind, however, that there are limits to the amount of stress we should subject ourselves to, as even the most antifragile structure will eventually break down beyond return. We are not looking to tear everything down. Therefore, keep the following two principles in mind to avoid emotional and physical burnout.

1. "It's not everything or nothing." Go for experiences that provide "some" stress or pressure: As a young athlete, you've got time on your side. Remember that even if you reach the pros at the early age of twenty-one, if you started learning a sport at six years old, then you've been training for 15 years! Emphasize the process and your plan for getting better rather than stressing so much about outcomes.

- Set short-, medium- and long-term goals and develop specific action steps to accomplish them. Sidestep overuse injuries and burnout by taking a day off each week and several weeks off each year. Stay involved in another sport or other fitness activities rather than specializing too early. Balance academics and sports with family, friends, and hobbies.

2. Rest and recovery to build: To maintain focus, you must manage your energy. Mini-breaks during the day are vital; this includes relaxation/breathing/stretching. The body repairs and builds during sleep, thus it is vital to get a good night of recuperative sleep. Don't catch up on sleep all on the weekend. Get regular sleep to build and refresh.

- For a good night's sleep to be possible, you can't just flip a switch. Take some time before sleeping to power down. This includes getting off the phone, ending gaming sessions, turning off other screens, and basically chilling out so that your body knows that sleep is coming.

In sum, strive to move along the continuum from fragile to robust to antifragile in all areas of your sport and life. Take a moment now to think about how you can become more and more antifragile in your approach. Everything is an opportunity to grow and get better. Game on!

ATTITUDE OVER ADVERSITY

*The absence of adversity is an indicator that
my goals aren't significant enough.*

—CLINT BRUCE,
FORMER NAVY SEAL AND FOOTBALL PLAYER

The main purpose of competitive sports is to test players beyond their perceived limits (i.e., pushing the boundaries). If you are lucky, you will be tested every day, so look forward to it. When you encounter the following types of adverse situations in your own game and life, vow to respond like a champion (do your best, take risks, and refuse to lose) and get back on a positive track toward accomplishing your big-picture goals.

ADVERSE SITUATION 1: Manning is a 15-year old basketball player who made the high-school team for the first time. He grew up playing with his older brothers and other kids in the neighborhood, and so this is his first experience in an organized program. Although active during practice games, he's been seen standing around during drills. He says, "I'm so bored with drills and practice, why can't we just play more games?"

CHAMPION'S RESPONSE: The coach talks to Manning and shows his appreciation for his talent, and then adds, "Manning, there's a purpose to practice, which is to learn new skills, lock in patterns, and learn about your teammates. This is important for winning games and growing and developing as a player, which I know is ultimately what you want to do. If we just play games all the time, sure it'll be fun, but we're not going to improve and certainly not win—especially against opponents who prepare better than we do. I want you to be a leader for the team and help me get everyone focused during practice, so that we can be our best this season."

ADVERSE SITUATION 2: Seventeen-year-old Jenny has been running track for several years and has made the division finals. This year, the coach asked her to implement a new weight-lifting conditioning program. After going through some intervals, she grew frustrated and said, "This is too hard, I don't think I really need this."

CHAMPION'S RESPONSE: Coach is talking with Jenny and asks her about her goals this season: Is she hoping to win the state meet, or is she trying to focus more on the Academic Olympiad, or is there anything else going on? Jenny says she wants to win the state meet and improve her personal times so that she can get a college scholarship. Later in the week, the coach comes back with some stats and shows them to Jenny. These are the Olympic, national, and state times in her events. He emphasizes to Jenny that her form and reaction off the blocks are great, but notes from the split times that she loses speed at about the midway point. He emphasizes that this is why she needs more strength. Realizing this, Jenny really starts to grunt out her strength-conditioning workouts.

ADVERSE SITUATION 3: Reggie plays both baseball and football and is into weight lifting. Lately, he seems a bit uninvolved and has spent more time listening to music and hanging out with his friends. The coach asks him about this, and Reggie responds by saying, "This isn't important to me."

CHAMPION'S RESPONSE: Coach takes Reggie out to a minor-league practice session. They have lunch and chat about how things are going. Coach says, "Reggie, I've known you since junior high and you've always put in one hundred percent, whether it's baseball, football, or other sports. But lately, you seem less interested. What's up?" Reggie answers, "My grandmother is getting old, and now sometimes she just yells at me and can't do stuff. It wasn't like before." Coach and Reggie talk about family, aging grandparents, finding your own life, and enjoying it to the maximum. Reggie decides to dedicate the season to his grandmother and writes her a note about how much he appreciates who she is and everything she has done for him.

ADVERSE SITUATION 4: Anthony has been running track for several years, but now, in his freshman year in high school, many of his competitors are older and he is getting beaten in races by higher margins. He is talking with his coach and says, "I might as well give up."

CHAMPION'S RESPONSE: Coach takes Anthony to a preschool, where they lead a group of kids in some games. Later, coach asks Anthony if he enjoyed that. Anthony says, "Yes, the kids are great. They run around and just laugh at everything." Coach asks, "Did any of them laugh at you?" Anthony says, "No, they just were playing. They kind of thought I was superman because I could do everything better than them." Coach says, "Are you better than them?" Anthony considers this and says, "No, I'm just older and bigger." Coach asks, "So should they give up and not try to play sports?" Anthony sips his sports drink, "Okay, Coach, I get it. Let's hit the sprints hard on Monday."

ADVERSE SITUATION 5: Tommy has been the star point-guard in high school since his sophomore year. He was one of the taller kids just after junior high, but in senior year, his teammates caught up in terms of height and game skills. His coach wants him to work harder on several new plays, but Tommy responds, "I'm just in a slump."

CHAMPION'S RESPONSE: Coach says, "Hey, Tommy, Larry can't seem to get the ball in the basket for an easy layup when you pass him the ball. We have a big game with Beaverton High in three weeks, and we lost to them last year. Go help him get out of his *slump*."

ADVERSE SITUATION 6: Josh is a great soccer player with a lot of natural talent. His parents aren't particularly involved in his sports, but they have high expectations for him both academically and in extracurricular activities. The coach has noticed that lately Josh seems to pull back on key plays toward the end of the game and he asks him about this. Josh says, "I can't handle failure, so I guess I'm just passing the ball rather than taking the ball downfield myself."

CHAMPION'S RESPONSE: Coach sits down with Josh and says, "Champions play to win. Failure is just feedback. There's everything to gain by trying your best. Now, let's go through your mental visualization script. Let me hear you say it. We're going to work on it and put together a schedule for rehearsing it."

ADVERSE SITUATION 7: Linda has been playing softball since Little League and is a powerful pitcher. She's got a lot of natural talent, and when she's on her game, she can really obliterate batters. This year, however, a couple of younger new players have come up and Linda is not starting games as often. She says to her coach, "I deserve to be the starter."

CHAMPION'S RESPONSE: Coach schedules a movie session for the team. It's a documentary on the run-up to the swimming competition for the Olympic tryouts. In the documentary there is a swimmer who eventually goes on to medal and a swimmer who doesn't make the team. In a competition, it is never certain who will win. There is only one certainty that is within your control: how much effort you put in.

ADVERSE SITUATION 8: Mika takes an aggressive serve-and-volley approach to tennis. She moves well on the court and usually overpowers her opponents. During some points, however, she throws her racquet and argues with opponents over close line calls. The coach pulls her aside after one particular tournament and asks about several incidents. Mika responds, "I don't like myself when I lose."

CHAMPION'S RESPONSE: Coach asks an assistant to watch a few of Mika's games and to video her outbursts and great shots. Later, they put together a montage and talk to Mika about what they're seeing. They go through some things she can do to check herself when she gets into an emotional situation, such as turning away from the opponent and taking three big breaths, counting the strings on her racquet, and saying something positive to herself.

ADVERSE SITUATION 9: Dylan has had his hopes on getting a wrestling scholarship, but he was sidelined this season with an ankle injury. The fitness coach puts him on a plan to do more workouts in the pool and focus more on upper-body workouts for the time being. However, his teammates came to the coach and said that lately Dylan has been really pissed off and is constantly arguing with everyone. When the coach asks Dylan about this news, he says, "I'm injured, and this sucks."

CHAMPION'S RESPONSE: Coach gives Dylan an assignment to research stories about elite athletes who've bounced back from injuries and asks him to write a paper on it.

ADVERSE SITUATION 10: Leslie is a star judo player in her division. She's got a lot of natural talent, works really hard, and is expected to go on to national finals this year. She's also on the Academic Olympiad and takes piano lessons. One day, her coach sees her on the mat seemingly in a daze and asks her about this. Leslie responds, "I don't have any time for a social life."

CHAMPION'S RESPONSE: Coach schedules a meeting with Leslie and her parents. They talk about finding the time to give Leslie an "off" day to rejuvenate and spend time with friends. Coach also brings in some stats and research about recovery time and shares some anecdotes about what some of the premier judo players do during their free time.

ADVERSE SITUATION 11: Jose comes back to the dugout screaming and throwing stuff around. He says, "I was screwed by that umpire."

CHAMPION'S RESPONSE: Coach says, "I appreciate your intensity, Jose. But remember that our goal as a team is to act like champions especially when things don't go our way. Let's take pride in doing that. So, take a breath, clap your hands, and flush away the at-bat. Now, get your head back in the game and go cheer on your teammates."

ADVERSE SITUATION 12: The girls' volleyball team has been on an exciting run this year to the divisional semifinals. However, they're up against the neighboring city's team, which they've already lost to twice this year. One of the girls says, "Coach, they've got two six-foot one-inch blockers, and they're all seniors. We can't beat them."

CHAMPION'S RESPONSE: Coach brings in the boys' team for a couple of practice sessions. They work on some plays to get around tall blockers. They also spend time visualizing successful execution of their game plan.

ADVERSE SITUATION 13: Francis is talking with his buddy Carl and says, "Coach doesn't like me."

CHAMPION'S RESPONSE: Carl responds, "Coach starts you every game. I'm sitting on the bench until the last quarter. Besides, he wasn't criticizing you at practice today. He was just giving you positive corrections because he knows how good you can be."

ADVERSE SITUATION 14: There are three squads for the field-hockey team. One is for first- and second-year students and focuses more on intramural matches. The other two are a junior varsity and varsity squad. These teams, however, often practice together because of limited field space. Jenny says to her mom, "My team-mates are so selfish and cliquish."

CHAMPION'S RESPONSE: Jenny's mom says, "Kids form cliques out of insecurity. Be the bigger person and the better team-mate. Bring the same positive attitude and best effort to practice each day and eventually they'll come around. So who do you sit with during lunch these days?"

ADVERSE SITUATION 15: There is a Parent-Teacher Association meeting and the discussion has turned to everyone's kids and social media. Mrs. Cortez, the mother of Nadia, who is on the tennis team, says, "People on social media are so mean, and Nadia has shown me some posts from other kids that are really mean."

CHAMPION'S RESPONSE: The PTA decides to put together a school policy on social media and begins discussions with the principal about current guidelines around the nation. Nadia has several options, such as saving and printing out the negative notes and using them as motivational fuel (and certainly not responding), closing her online accounts and opening new ones with a different user name, and blocking people sending harassing notes.

ADVERSE SITUATION 16: Leilei is a nationally ranked short-distance swimmer. She is in the pool at 6:00 a.m. before classes start and returns to the pool in the afternoons. It's the start of her senior year and the coach is talking about how they can move toward hitting her personal best times this year. Leilei seems distracted and eventually says, "I'm worried about whether I'll get an athletic scholarship."

CHAMPION'S RESPONSE: Coach applies the end-of-the-world approach and asks Leilei, "So what happens if you don't get an athletic scholarship?" Leilei responds, "I don't know, I guess I'd have to work part-time while going to school." Coach says, "You know, most swimmers trying to qualify for the Olympics are working part time to support their training. I don't think that will stop you." Leilei thinks about this, "Yes, I guess I can work flexible hours at a coffee shop."

ADVERSE SITUATION 17: Ronnie has been a great baseball player all through Little League and junior high. He excels at focusing during practice, and his teammates value that a lot. Lately, however, it seems that even he is putting less effort into practices. The coach asks him about this and Ronnie responds, "I'm too far behind others in my sport to be as good as they are."

CHAMPION'S RESPONSE: Coach asks Ronnie, "I've known you for a long time, so let me ask you something: Why do you play baseball?" Ronnie says, "I like playing with the other guys." Coach says, "Some of them are playing better than you." Ronnie says, "Yes, but we're a team." Coach says, "That's right, Ronnie: we're a team, and we all put in one hundred percent during practices. We need you to do that for our team."

ADVERSE SITUATION 18: Ever since he was seven years old, Oscar has had everything. His dad is a CEO and his mom runs a nonprofit. They have encouraged him to be involved in a lot of activities and have always given him opportunities to explore and try out new things. He's in his junior year now, and his coach on the basketball team is talking to him about off-season practices this summer before his senior year. Oscar says, "I don't need to work hard now. I'll turn it on during my senior year."

CHAMPION'S RESPONSE: Coach asks Oscar to come over and watch some videos in the media room. They sit and watch Michael Jordan, Larry Bird, and Magic Johnson footage from high school, college, and then the NBA. Coach eventually asks Oscar, "When did these guys 'turn it on?'" Oscar says, "I don't think they had it turned off."

ADVERSE SITUATION 19: This is the first time for Matthew to play in a post-season hockey match. During practice, he says to the coach, "I'm so nervous about the big game."

CHAMPION'S RESPONSE: The coach tells Matthew, "There's nothing like experience to make you better. The puck doesn't change just because of the date, time, or place. A champion will stay focused on the present. This is done both at practices and on game day. Go through your normal routines to calm the jitters. Do some sprints during warm-up to wake up your heart and prepare your body. Take some deep breaths. In your mental imagery, win the point, challenge the situation, and be your best. Most importantly, think about how much fun we're going to have!"

ADVERSE SITUATION 20: Melody is a water polo player. She has three sisters who are also all involved in sports and volunteer activities at Division 1 schools. Lately, Melody seems to have tuned out and is uncommunicative.

CHAMPION'S RESPONSE: A higher purpose is necessary to prioritize, select, motivate, and gain or maintain perspective. This is the time for Melody to step away and look at the overall situation. Like a champion might turn to a mentor, a trusted friend, or a new environment to reflect on things, Melody can do the same. It might be time for her to do some volunteer work at a hospital, help some children with after-school activities, or visit with relatives—something that doesn't involve sports directly. When Melody gains a better perspective on her goals, she can come back and start re-engaging with her core activities.

ADVERSE SITUATION 21: Brad is a gifted college golfer who dreams of becoming a professional on tour. He grew up with all of the benefits of the country-club life: private golf lessons, top-of-the-line equipment, and many trips to school and individual tournaments statewide. He's happy with his skill level as he often wins, but he has yet to defeat a rival college player named Jack. This failure to win has resulted in Brad being unable to win against Jack for two reasons: his concentration on Jack's game rather than on his own and his loss of temper, whereas Jack seems cool, especially under pressure (he's already beaten Brad in three playoffs). Brad knows Jack came from a low-income family and had to work at a course in exchange for lessons and free range balls. His clubs are not customized. Brad's reasoning is that if he cannot beat Jack locally, then how can he win anything nationally or internationally on the tour in the future?

CHAMPION'S RESPONSE: After watching Brad falter and lose a fourth playoff to Jack, his coach sits him down in the clubhouse. Brad is clearly frustrated. Coach says, "Brad, you've got the physical skills to beat Jack, but not the mental ones. You beat yourself. Also, you probably don't know that Jack practices every day and sometimes twice a day on the weekends before and after his job. His coach told me that Jack reads every golf book or magazine he can find. In short, he's outworking and outlearning you. I can help you set up a stricter, more disciplined work schedule, but you're responsible for following it. I'm not guaranteeing that you will beat Jack, but you will force him to up his game to keep beating you."

ADVERSE SITUATION 22: Todd is a star athlete at his high school. He's student council president and a national merit scholar. Things have been easy for him so far, but lately he's been preoccupied with what his peers think. Sometimes his friends want to goof off, but he knows that means missing practice or spending less time on his homework. He wants to fit in and have friends. These days, he tends to showboat during a game to get attention.

CHAMPION'S RESPONSE: Coach pulls him aside one day and says, "Todd, you've got to step up and lead. A champion knows that there are a lot of distractions and conflicting priorities in today's world. There are also others who will pull you down for their own short-term gain. They are not looking out for you! Instead of letting other distractions creep into your work ethic and attitude, make sure to take some time to reflect and sharpen the bigger picture. Are you working for acceptance to a highly ranked school program? Are you aiming to beat state records in your sport? Are you developing friends that support and lift you up? In other words, are you responding to various distractions by becoming more or less focused?"

THE ANTIFRAGILE TEAM

I've always made a total effort, even when the odds seemed entirely against me. I never quit trying; I never felt that I didn't have a chance to win.

—ARNOLD PALMER

Head coach Gary Gilmore of Coastal Carolina University baseball started emphasizing the field between the ears with his players through a mental conditioning program and they eventually made it to the NCAA tournament in 2016.

The Chanticleers' amazing, thrilling run to glory included facing five elimination games in the tournament, knocked off higher-ranked teams, and pulled off the "Miracle on Dirt" with their incredible win over Arizona in the finals. This was their first time in the tournament and they went all the way.

This was a great underdog story and many people were happy for Coach Gilmore—21 years of coaching and now he had the best paperweight ever for his desk: the NCAA championship trophy.

In fact, it is a classic case study. How did the boys from the swamp (which is most of Horry County, South Carolina) win a national championship? The coach said it best: "We're not the most talented team. We're just the national champions."

So it had to be a simple belief—some alchemy. Maybe what the alchemists were looking for wasn't a solid metal, but a spiritual mettle that turned lead into NCAA gold for Coastal Carolina.

Of the five times they faced elimination, once was with only one out to go. One swing, one hope (the South Carolina motto is *Dum spiro spero*, which is Latin for "While I breathe, I hope"). Sure, they had good luck and a bad call (the Arizona kid was safe at home, so the game should have been tied). The point is that champions want the chance, no matter the outcome.

In the middle of the players' home locker room, there's a cordoned-off area with a mat on the floor. On the mat, there's a chanticleer with the words *selfless* and *relentless*. The only time a player is allowed to be in the cordoned-off area is with the coach and as the player of the game after a win.

In your own game and life, stay selfless (team player) and relentless (keep going) in your quest to be your best. Learning and using the tools and techniques outlined in this book will help propel you on your journey toward your own "miracle" performance, in your own way, at your own time, and on your own playing field.

But it all starts with always believing in yourself (champion's mind). Play the game between the ears and be the winner of it!

FINISH LINE

Contemporary society, and actually, history, is very much focused on achievements and one-off events. For example, winning the

Super Bowl, landing on the moon, or a landmark law being passed. While there is no doubt that these are wonderful accomplishments, it is important to realize that they are just mile markers on a long highway. Leading up to any Super Bowl there were preseason, season, and post-season games. The athletes on that Super Bowl-winning team had injuries, they lost, they struggled, and only at the end of that did they become Super Bowl champions. The road was long! Looking down this long stretch of highway, you cannot have a small gas tank. You cannot be fragile.

You have to be antifragile. There has to be a lot in the tank. The tank must be big. It means that with every problem that you encounter, you get amped up to challenge it, to solve it, to grow from it, all toward a higher goal. Think about the huge team of engineers, mathematicians, managers, and astronauts that took humanity to the moon. How many problems, setbacks, and just plain old situations of fear did they face? How good were they at working together as a team to think and do things that had never been done before? What made them antifragile?

Accomplishing big things, becoming a champion—in some ways it's like being a nine-headed hydra or lizard that grows back a bigger tail. You have to have an ingrained, learned, genetic—call it what you want—ability to take a challenge and come back with more. That's what you want to have, the ability to come back with more! When you give more, you usually get back plus some.

CHAPTER FOUR

PLAYING IN THE ZONE

Once you've tasted the heavens, you walk the earth with
upturned eyes, for you have been there and long to return.

—LEONARDO DA VINCI

Zone or flow states are states of mind that happen when people stop overthinking and start trusting. A person becomes almost lost in the moment, and this usually happens when people are performing at their peak while doing their chosen activity. A very influential book called *Finding Flow*, by a psychology researcher named Mihaly Csikszentmihalyi, was one of the first to describe this state.

The zone is when all the invisible connections are strengthened between a person and the task being performed. This is a state of mind that we're all looking for! The activity becomes pure, and its essence emerges. An activity becomes boxed in, and everything else is boxed out. Everything seems to slow down. Time (clock time) no longer is a part of the equation, while timing (i.e., performing the task) becomes paramount.

Could this particular state help to explain what separates elite athletes from others? How would those who have mastered their sport describe the zone? Most of them say they are calm and focused on the task at hand. There isn't incessant attention to the score or fear about negative eventualities. In fact, the zone is a blissful place where body and mind became one. Listen to two-time NBA MVP Stephen Curry describing his experience playing in the zone:

> The game is slow. It just feels so comfortable, smooth, natural. It's the confidence that when we're out on the floor, only good things are gonna happen. Any move you wanna make, it happens. You'll miss shots, but there's a flow to everything you do. It's cool. I'm on cloud nine.

Eleven-time NBA champion Bill Russell described his own "cloud nine" experiences in his memoir, *Second Wind*:

> Every so often a Celtics game . . . would be magical. That feeling is difficult to describe, and I certainly never talked about it when I was playing. When it happened, I could feel my play rise to a new level. It came rarely, and would last anywhere from five minutes to a whole quarter, or more. . . . The game would move so quickly that every fake, cut, and pass would be surprising, and yet nothing could surprise me. It was almost as if we were playing in slow motion. During those spells, I could almost sense how the next play would develop and where the next shot would be taken. . . . There have been many times in my career when I felt moved or joyful, but these were the moments when I had chills pulsing up and down my spine.

Frequently, athletes explain their zone occurrences as "blacking out." Here's Carli Lloyd on her epic midfield goal and hat trick that led USA to a 5 to 2 victory against defending World Cup champion Japan in the 2015 championship game:

> I've dreamed of scoring a shot like that. When you're feeling good mentally, physically, those plays just are instincts and it just happens. I feel like I *blacked out* the first 30 minutes or so in that game.

Likewise, Tiger Woods in his prime talked on *Golf Channel* about "blacking out" over shots in tournament play:

> I tend to have these blackout moments where I don't remember. I know I was there, but I don't remember actually performing the golf shot. I'd get so entrenched in the moment, my subconscious takes over. There are many putts and many shots I don't remember hitting. I remember seeing the ball flight, I remember preparing for the shot, but once I walk into the shot, I don't remember until I see the ball leave. For some reason, the last few holes [of a tournament] take forever. They may be happening faster, but they seem to be taking a long time. I don't hear noise, I don't hear anything. I'm just enthralled in that moment.

For five-time NBA champion Kobe Bryant, "blackout" means total focus in the moment:

> Blackout is an attitude. It's a way of life. No matter what it is that you do. I don't care if you're a carpenter, a basketball player, a doctor, doesn't matter. You focus 100 percent on what you're doing in that moment, nothing else matters. That's what blackin' out means to me.

The zone is obvious in tennis if you listen carefully because the ball *sounds* different leaving the racquet when the motions of your body are fluid, linked, and precise. Your shots go to where you want them to go without consciously aiming. A tennis player knows they are hitting well when they have moved into the proper position, timed the ball perfectly, and a beautiful sound resonates as the ball leaves the racquet. It all happens fast, and hitting the racquet sweet spot shot is a sign that you are either in or near the zone.

In sports, it is almost as if the ultimate goal (e.g., victory) fades away when one enters the zone. This is like when a top golfer doesn't look at the leaderboard and just focuses on the simple goal of "ball in the hole." The mind becomes closely attuned to what the body is doing, and consequently there is no disconnection between reflex, muscle action, and motivation. Instead, there is the perfect alignment of stimuli, body, and target.

Flow can happen with any activity, not just sports. Flow can be experienced in every activity, be it art or a business negotiation. For example, if a painter is really engrossed in an art project, she can feel her mind moving quickly while maintaining focus. She loses awareness of time and an hour flies seemingly like a minute. There is unity between the "images" in her mind and the movement of her paintbrush on the canvas.

Neurologically, what's happening in the flow state is that activation changes in specific parts of the brain, with some parts becoming activated more strongly while others become less activated. As activity in the frontal lobe decreases, the volume of inner chatter or inner voice—"the narrator" who is always speaking to us—is turned down or off. This minimizes or eliminates chatter about the past and future. What remains? The present.

Interestingly, we can see the impact of these areas of the brain when disease strikes. For example, in order to assess brain functions in Alzheimer's patients, clinicians ask these patients to tell time ("What year is it?"), count backwards, and to consciously remember objects and pieces of information. The questioner is testing for memory/recall after a short period of time has passed and for "executive" cognitive function. In *My Stroke of Insight: A Brain Scientist's Personal Journey*, author Jill Bolte Taylor talks about a "bliss" state, a feeling of contentment after parts of her brain shut down after a stroke.

Conscious processing is performing by the frontal lobe, while more automatic processes are performed by other brain areas. In other neurological studies, researchers looked at awareness versus conscious thought. Specifically, the researchers were looking at the processing of familiar versus unfamiliar faces. They wanted to know to what extent the brain is able to process outside stimuli beyond the bounds of conscious thought. In this activity, the frontal lobe appears to do much of the conscious processing. A type of imaging system called fMRI was used to see what brain sections were being activated. Awareness, automatic responses, cognitive function activate different areas of the brain.

While we utilize our frontal/executive function processing for some activities, other parts of our brain are engaged in different unconscious, automatic activities. Many of our daily tasks would be impossible without such unconscious processing. We don't need to think consciously about driving, or how to pick up a spoon, or even be aware of the mechanics of walking. These sorts of activities have become so ingrained that conscious thought doesn't usually get involved, and instead the patterns have become automatic.

In the past, such patterns, which utilize more primal parts of the brain located near the back of the head, allowed us to survive, eat, and react in a world that could be navigated more instinctually. In today's world, however, modern people utilize this part of the brain much less, with sports being one of the few opportunities to "not think" about doing something. The body and brain are simply doing. This is one reason why sports can be so engaging and enjoyable.

How does one get the flow going? Consider teaching tennis to a beginner and explaining how to learn a stroke by sometimes breaking it down to build proper muscle memory. While this sort of learning and practice is necessary, it is also important to have activities where one can just "let it all go," such as by focusing on some fun exercises that involve game play and targets, rather than explicitly defined muscle-movement patterns.

Letting it all flow is often a hard concept to convey to others, maybe because it has to come from within oneself. While some people are "thinkers" and prefer to analyze everything, others dislike all instructions and *just want to hit the ball*. Typically, though, the "doers" end up flailing away at their sport. Learning takes a mix of thinking and flowing.

Alternatively, one practice technique is to ask a player to focus on where they want the ball to go and its flight path, and then adjust the racquet's motion accordingly, rather than focusing on a specific aspect of the swing (backswing, impact, or follow-through). This provides a combination of approaches and allows for some focused practice.

When in the proper state of a flowing mind, you are able to execute an action, a skilled movement, with both intention and feeling. Things are clicking into place. Even a great athlete like Michael Jordan sometimes juked, jived, contorted, and appeared to force shots—and then his shot dropped, mission accomplished. The mind-body movements flowed.

The joy of flow is why people like to play sports. There is an opportunity to get into the zone, and to become free from all worries about daily life and the stresses from a thinking mind. Flow is the runner's high. Why else would anyone want to run for miles and miles, except to experience the flow that generates the high?

There is also something primal about making good contact with a ball. I've seen kids and adults, on the driving range or in the batting cage, just plain happy about making good contact. In fact, some athletes enjoy training for golf tournaments or baseball games more than playing in them. In the back of their minds, they are improving their games, but to them practicing is also enjoyable for its own sake. Keep this in mind when you're dreading practice.

Time is another key element. Looking back, when were you in the zone? It's a moment in which the player got out of the way of training and practice. The passage of time gives way to action/reaction. Reflection about what is happening gives way to pinpoint perception about what is happening. Maybe most important, the future becomes available in the now as you anticipate, see, and respond before things have happened, without conscious thought.

A word of caution: the harder you try to force your way into the zone, the more elusive it is. So what is a perfect target for entering the zone? What helps you get there? Interestingly, some of the best methods are off the field. Consider the following guidelines for producing the zone:

• **Set the conditions for a good night's sleep**. If you try to force yourself to sleep, you will become wider awake. The key is to develop habits and practices so that you are sleeping well on a consistent basis: for example, turning down the lights at night and practicing deep breathing.

• **Watch a good movie that makes you cry or laugh**. All the necessary conditions are there to become immersed in the world of a movie. You are there with the characters, and your emotions rise and fall with their story. Each movie will affect each individual differently. Find out what type of movie suits your mood.

• **Enjoy good cooking**. You can put all the ingredients and the same recipe on a counter, but the end result will differ depending on who cooks: a novice, an experienced cook, or a five-star Michelin chef. Know thyself and what you like to eat.

With all the above said about what the zone is, many players of all sports will want to know if it is possible to replicate a triumphant state of mind spontaneously at any given moment. It is. Just study what high-performance athletes said about this and much more as they recollected their zone moments. Annika Sorenstam shot the lowest round in LPGA Tour history by firing a 59 during the second round of the 2001 Safeway International. She recounted her historic round on *Golf Channel*:

> I wasn't worrying about anything. I would stand on the tee; I would just swing it. I would stand on the fairway; I was just trying to hit the green. I wasn't worrying where the ball was going; same thing on my putting, I wasn't worrying about my second putt. I was just looking at the hole and that is what I was concerned about. I was so free in my mind, there was no excess or whatever you call it around me.

In addition to staying in the moment and focusing less on results and more on the process to get there, here are some additional zone "ingredients" to consider:

• **Cultivate an attitude of gratitude.** Appreciate your teammates, coaches, parents, and fans. Playing sports at any level provides the privilege of just being on a team. A life of gratitude leads to greatness. You'll compete better because you will be emotionally free.

• **Practice mindfulness meditation.** Practice quieting your mind away from the field (court, course) to help you develop a focused, uncluttered mind on the field.

• **Be deliberate in training.** Focus on high-quality reps in training to sharpen your focus. Practice also needs to mimic the adrenaline and rush of true competition. Don't just go through the motions. It's vital to practice a competitive mind-set.

• **Establish performance routines.** A proper plan of attack allows you to get in the right frame of mind and rhythm to perform.

• **Challenge yourself.** See competition as a challenge to meet rather than a threat to avoid. Once the game begins, feel your body and intuition take over. Enjoy the focus that comes with game speed. Trust in your training and talent.

• **Use your creative imagination.** Visualize in high-definition what you want to happen, rather than thinking about too many technicalities.

• **Slow down.** The best advice for managing perceived pressure is to slow down. Think slower, breathe slower, and walk slower.

• **Bring it back to simple.** Keep performance as simple as possible. As MLB Hall of Famer Willie Mays said, "They throw the ball, I hit it. They hit the ball, I catch it."

• **Enjoy the joy.** In the end, it's a game, so have fun. Besides, the more fun you have, the better you will perform. The better you perform, the more fun you will have.

In terms of specific practice and preparation for sports, ask yourself the following self-reflection questions:

• Do I have a solid and repeatable pregame routine to get myself into the zone for a game? If not, why not?

• How have I found my way into the zone? Was I more diligent about pregame warm-ups or about techniques used during a game?

• What phrases or words do I use during competition to remind myself that I may be overthinking and underperforming?

• How did I respond to external factors, people, and conditions when I was playing a match? Did my response get me closer to the zone or just into stressed-out cognitive thinking and worrying?

The zone is as old as Zen: calm your mind, set aside all thoughts of "if," "but," and "maybe." Accept that you don't know the outcome yet and only act/react. The act part comes from inspiration and the reaction is automatic and without thought. In contrast, choking, feeling off rhythm, and getting frustrated typically come from overthinking and not being.

Here's how a friend described a zone experience he had while playing tennis. "Warmed up, played the match, crushed my opponent, who had beaten me several weeks earlier, and then he said, 'You can take off your warm-up jacket now.' Never crossed my mind during the warm-up, the match, or the aftermath. Toss the ball on the serve, hit to a spot, charge the net, volley hard, and stay alert to volley harder. I beat him in two sets in about forty-five minutes, this after a long three-setter in the first match." That's the zone!

Another friend's zone experience occurred one August on two weekends, when he broke par on the same course. He said, "I swung easy, made a lot of putts, didn't worry about the score, and enjoyed the afternoon." But here's the amazing part. After shooting 71 that weekend, he went to the same course the next weekend, and didn't let the previous weekend affect the moment. In fact, he had a putt on 18 to score 69 and didn't know it until after he'd made it. His playing partner asked, "You did know you had to make that putt to break seventy, didn't you?" My friend said, "No." He treated it like every other putt in the round, up and in.

I like formulas, so here's one for the zone:

Moment – past experiences (good or bad) + opportunities – all thoughts of previous opportunities + a deep breath and a smile to recognize PLAYING a game = acceptance of the outcome.

ZONE is an acronym for "Z" (the moment, stupid) + ONE (you). To be in the zone is to be in the moment. If you think, "I'm in the zone," you're not, because you've taken the reflection step, which puts you out of the zone. Reflection is one step forward out of the zone, where you realize you were in the zone. If lucky, you'll step back into nonthinking.

Each player has the only key to their OWN Z-own. So, another thought along this same line is Z-one, meaning, as above, you are the only ONE who can find your zone. External factors (opponent, their gamesmanship in actions or remarks, the crowd's reaction, the weather, etc.) are irrelevant and mere distractions. Internal factors are critical (silencing the voice of doubt, hesitation, the what-if's, etc.). The key to Z-one is that you're the only one—when you are calm, trusting your preparation, and confident that you can flow with whatever happens.

What elements can pop the zone bubble? Some might say the roar of the crowd (football) or the total silence (golf). Most will, however, cite internal factors as the biggest possible distraction. The mind can easily start to obsess about some miscellaneous thought or start to analyze a situation. In a competition, or with fast moving events, the mind-body needs to focus on the task and not the past or future. While external factors have a "null" effect, internal factors can result in either triumph or disaster.

Zone
Interview

Dr. Christian Swann is currently a sport psychology researcher at the University of Wollongong, Australia, working on a mental health project in youth sport. His dissertation was on the occurrence of flow in elite golfers, which included European Tour and Ryder Cup players. He's accredited with the British Association of Sport and Exercise Sciences and has consulted with athletes and teams across a range of ages, sports, and levels. He describes himself as a big fan of most sports—particularly soccer, rugby, and golf—and plays a few different sports at the moment (without being very good at any of them, he jokes). Here's my interview with Dr. Swann:

Q: What attracted you to having a professional career in sport psychology?

A: I've been fascinated by sport psychology from a young age. I played golf competitively and became interested in Bob Rotella's books as a way of trying to improve my game. By trying out some of the ideas in those books, I learned about how psychology plays a huge role in sport performance and in getting more out of ourselves generally. From there, I did a sports degree at university and chose to focus on sport psychology wherever I could.

Q: Can you describe some of your own personal flow experiences in your own sports participation?

A: My strongest experiences of flow happened while I was playing golf at university in England. I remember a couple of occasions when I performed as well as I possibly could, and the experience felt relaxed, effortless, easy, and like my main job was to stay out of my own way! These experiences often happened when I was playing against much better players (and holding my own!) or in important rounds of golf like trials for the university team. Through these experiences I became really interested in understanding how/why they occur, and how to help other athletes get into flow more often.

Q: What are your favorite examples or stories of flow from professional sports?

A: As a golfer, some of my favorite examples of flow came from Tiger Woods in his prime. In the late 2000s, he was playing so well it really seemed like no one else had a chance. There are too many examples from his career to highlight one in particular, but I certainly enjoyed watching him and hearing him describe his experiences of flow in interviews afterwards. More generally, tennis matches are usually a great arena for seeing players in flow, and it's amazing how much sets and matches can swing. As a recent example, the 2017 Australian Open final between Roger Federer and Rafa Nadal was exceptional and as a spectator you could almost see when each player was experiencing flow during the match (which Roger ultimately won in the 5th set).

Q: What are some of the early sport-psychology research studies on flow or playing in the zone?

A: Some of the earliest research on the psychology of peak performance was conducted by Ken Ravizza (1977, 1984). A bit later, Susan Jackson conducted the first research applying Csikszentmihalyi's model of flow in sport (1992, 1995, 1996). Some of these studies are still very popular today, and these researchers really led the way for research into flow and the zone in sport.

Q: What are the key findings from these investigations?
A: The key findings from these early studies focused on describing athletes' experiences of being in flow (Jackson, 1995) and the factors associated with the occurrence of flow (Jackson, 1992, 1996). Key findings initially were that Csikszentmihalyi's model of flow seemed to apply in sport and that athletes reported similar characteristics of flow as in other domains (Jackson, 1996). These early studies also found that things like a positive attitude, physical readiness, and maintaining appropriate focus were associated with the occurrence of flow (Jackson, 1992, 1995). These initial studies on flow in sport provided a foundation which researchers have continued to build on for over 20 years.

Q: Can you tell us about recent studies, including from your own lab?
A: Our recent studies (Swann et al., 2016, 2017a, 2017b) have interviewed athletes soon after they've had an excellent performance, like running a PB [personal best]. These studies have told us that athletes don't just experience flow—but that clutch states also play a big role in performing at our peak. A lot of research to date has been focused on flow, so finding out about clutch states opens up a lot of new angles to study. Interestingly, it seems like athletes can transition between flow and clutch states in the same performance, which means that it's important to understand how they both occur, and how athletes can manage them both in different ways. These are the key things we're currently working on.

Q: How does flow differ from clutch states?

A: Flow and clutch states involve a number of similarities, like being totally absorbed in the performance, feeling in control, and losing track of time. However, flow feels easy, effortless and automatic—whereas athletes in clutch states feel like they put in much more effort and try as hard as they can. In flow, our concentration on the task just seems to happen naturally, whereas in clutch states it's like we're really trying or forcing ourselves to concentrate on the task. Clutch states occur when we feel like we're under pressure and have to "step it up," but flow occurs when we aren't aware of pressure and are more interested in trying something new, experimenting, or exploring our limits. The type of goal we pursue also seems to be different: in clutch states we chase very specific goals (like making birdie on the last hole to win a golf tournament), but in flow we chase exploratory goals, like "seeing how many under par I can get."

Q: What are practical applications from the scientific literature for athletes seeking flow and clutch states?

A: By working on flow and clutch states, we're aiming to be able to identify key things that coaches and athletes can do in order to perform better more consistently. We want to provide clearer guidance on how to use specific strategies (like goal setting) in the right way to experience flow or clutch states when the situation is right. By being able to manage how these states occur, athletes and coaches will be able to get more out of themselves and maybe even achieve new levels of performance. Importantly, we're also interested in the psychological outcomes of flow and clutch states, so that we can help athletes push themselves in sport without risking stress, burnout, or even dropout.

FINISH LINE

In conclusion, to bring this all together, we are reminded how important joy is to sport. Specifically, much of the nonthinking, ingrained, and automatic engagement in sport is reflected by what many people call the zone. This is a mental space where cognitive thinking is mostly secondary, and instead our more primal, more responsive, and more automatic responses engage. In the contemporary world, we often have few moments to enjoy such thrills.

Therefore, in sport especially, it is important to acknowledge, learn, and also set free this zone. There are specific methods, reminders, and practices that can help us get into and stay in the zone. There are concepts like Z-OWN, or Z-one, that put a formula to this experience. However, it might be that you prefer to just get into the game and let it all go!

CHAPTER FIVE

VISUALIZATION ON THE GO

I am a big believer in visualization. I run through my races mentally so that I feel even more prepared.

—ALLYSON FELIX

isualization enables you to see victory and then win. Visualization, if consistently practiced, makes you mentally and physically primed for competition. This powerful tool maximizes what only you can control: your own mind. For example, play real fantasy baseball by imagining pitching out of a bases-loaded, two-out jam or coming through in the clutch by driving in the game-winning run.

When you visualize, make it as lifelike as possible and *decide what you want the outcome to be.* Become aware of your thoughts and feelings once you're in the outcome you want. With regular and structured practice, your imagery will become so vivid and controllable that you can feel your heart rate rise and the sweat on your forehead. When your heart rate rises, you know you're *in the moment.* Pause to breathe slowly and deeply to lower your heart rate and bring a calmness throughout your body.

Have you ever been onstage? Do you think that actors get in front of hundreds without a worry on their mind or a pang in their stomach? Of course not! They rehearse their roles frequently, and then go through a dress rehearsal followed by a final rehearsal and a stage check. Backstage before showtime, they take a few moments to gear up. In other words, they go through a ton of visualization. You need to do this, too.

Rehearse different scenarios, whether for peak performance or for triumphing over game-day adversity. Remember, if you still have one pitch, one swing, one shot, you still have a chance. In your mental preparation, get as many reps as you possibly can in this high-quality way of putting yourself through both favorable and unfavorable situations. Take note of the details and create the details *you want*. Imagine the slippery grass on the field and the creaking of bleacher seats as fans fill up the gym—*be aware of your surroundings*. You're onstage and on the field against other highly skilled opponents in challenging conditions—and you love all of it. Use imagery to prepare yourself to take advantage of a moment's opportunity (one throw, one swing, one shot).

This chapter provides you with some concrete tools, such as guided visualization scripts for several sports. You can use these scripts as is, or as a model to create your own personalized scripts. Make each an Oscar-winning performance.

Practice imagery in your living room, during downtime before practice, or in your room the night before a competition—long before you step onto the field, the course, or the court. Unlike physical practice, there's no injury risk and no physical exertion involved when you visualize. Think of it as building and ingraining patterns in your mind that you can reenact instinctively in game-day situations.

One suggestion is to read your script aloud as you record it on your smartphone so it's in your own voice. This will engage your mind much more than reading from a printed sheet. Listen to the script 2 or 3 times per week, or whenever you need a boost. Perhaps do this prior to practice, the night before a game, or during any downtime in your day. Listening to the audio with your headphones can be convenient during a plane flight, on the school bus, or on your way to a game. Just make sure you're not the one behind the wheel!

Here are the guided visualization scripts:

1. Golf

2. Tennis

3. Basketball

4. Soccer

5. Volleyball

6. Cross-Country

7. Cycling

8. Hockey

9. Baseball/Softball

10. American Football

11. Gymnastics

GUIDED VISUALIZATION: GOLF

Imagine lying down in a park or the backyard on a quiet, sunny day. Feel the sun's heat on your forehead as all your tension melts away. The sunlight pours onto your eyelids, which become heavy with warmth. Sense the energy of the sunshine in your entire body. The sunlight rolls down your shoulders and through your back as it begins to relax. Breathe deeply. With every breath you are filled with light and warmth. In this stillness you are calm and comfortable. Enjoy this moment.

Visualize arriving at the golf course for an important tournament—this final round means a lot to you because you are a competitor and now is the time to play your best. Feel totally powerful and unstoppable; be happy that you are a great player destined to be a champion. Feel the satisfaction: after thousands of hours of practice the here and now is, well, now.

In the locker room or maybe the parking lot, as you change into your golf shoes, you also change into a champion golfer. Your body feels strong and centered. Walk to the practice range and enjoy the crowd and your fellow golfers. Absorb the energy and the excitement of competition. Smile at your friends and family. After warming up, you walk to the first hole—it's time to play.

Concentrate on this shot; stay in the present. Focus only on your target and smash a drive down the middle of the fairway. Stride confidently to your ball. Hit a good-looking pin seeker, then drain the putt.

Your game plan is now an action plan. The targets and putting lines look bigger and brighter today. Your swing feels effortless. You are swinging in rhythm with terrific tempo. You are enjoying the simplicity of playing great golf.

Prepare for the next shot, the next target. You let the swing happen and the ball catapults off the clubface. You relax into the follow-through and look up. Your shot goes exactly as envisioned. The oldest cliché, to play one shot at a time, is the oldest for good reason: it's the truth. Forget past shots and rounds and just focus on how good it feels right now—win or lose—to be great.

Your opponents cannot pressure you, as only you can apply and either accept or reject that pressure. Forget them and enjoy the simplicity of the game. Allow your body to do what you have trained it to do. You know what you did to prepare. Could you have done more? Sure, if you had given up sleep and sanity. But you did what you could and now you accept that rest is as important as practice. A rested mind is ready to let you be you.

Know that you are strong physically, mentally, and emotionally, avoiding the hazards of fear and doubt. Nothing bothers or upsets you. You may miss a shot or two or more and will react the same: next shot, best shot. Each shot is the first shot of a new round. Be committed to the simplicity of "see it; hit it" all day long.

In between shots, you breathe slowly and chat with your caddie or playing partners, feeling free and loose—this is where you want to stay. If you miss a fairway or a green, you are not bothered in the least because you have a solid short game. Accept the shot because you can get up and down from anywhere. You know that every putt is yours to make. You walk up to the ball, thinking only about knocking it into the hole.

On the putting green, you see the line, see the ball, and watch it roll into the cup. Focus on how smooth your stroke feels and then putt fearlessly, like you did when playing a childhood game. Be that kid again. You have trained for this moment, so now play this game. Simple? Yes. Let simplicity stay simple. It is only hard if you make it hard.

Expect something good to happen—look for the good bounce, the putt to lip in. When you get a bad break, take it in stride. You know you are well prepared and destined to do big things this year. This is the game you are most talented at playing, the game you love and enjoy playing and winning.

Think about your love of the game and reflect on your only goal: see the shot, hit the target. Then see the line and sink the putt. What else matters? Accept that the simple answer is simply nothing. Each shot is a fresh shot. Commit to each shot with total trust in your preparation and your talent. Let the ball go where you want it to go—forcing is failing.

You have infinite patience because you have a calm mind. You already know that a consistent mental approach—shot by shot, all day every day—allows your training to let you win. The keys to scoring are simple, so don't make them hard: one shot a time, allow the swing to happen, accept the results, then repeat, repeat, repeat.

Your mind is silent as you stand over the ball. Focus only on your target. You enjoy trusting your instincts and allowing the flow. Let the other players overthink their club selection or obsess about their mechanics while you have fun just trusting yourself, loving your game, and enjoying your feelings.

On the putting green, trust your instinct to see the line and roll the ball into the cup, as instinct is true every time even when distrust often fails. Practice has sharpened your instincts. You trust your eagle eyes and go with your first impression. You soften your grip pressure for maximum feel and then release the blade.

There will be unexpected course conditions. Play can be slow sometimes, so let your opponents complain and get uptight. Ignore them and stay in your own *zone*. All day, all round, however long it takes, just have fun. Having fun is the prelude to your best performance. Your mind is in control, not the conditions. A still and quiet mind is your competitive edge.

You spend the round seeing the target and hitting it. Love the challenge of accepting the simplicity of you, one target, and your purpose. Nothing else matters. As your play improves, you get calmer. With each well-executed pre-shot routine, just let go and enjoy the next shot.

Let the *zone* come to you. It will if you simplify by letting your training, intuition, and athleticism take over. You are golfing, which is a form of playing. So be a player for the sheer joy of playing. You see clearly that golf is game to be played well by you.

On the 18th green, a well-struck iron shot leaves you a six-foot putt for birdie. You know that if you make it you win the tournament. Tell yourself that your final putt is the same as your first-shot goal: Trust with a quiet mind. You already are a champion. If you stay focused on every shot, then you will inevitably win your share of tournaments. See, feel, and trust as you roll the ball into the cup yet again.

As accolades pour over you, just smile and give high fives. Enjoy receiving and hoisting the trophy. Listen to your family and friends cheer. All of this is enjoyable, but pause to ponder how relaxed you were from the first tee to the last putt, how much fun you had, and how much trust you had in your skills.

You expect more days like this one because you are going to keep golf simple. Why? Because having fun is to see and do, and then success just happens. This is the best strategy for playing the game. Anything you can envision is possible and doable. If you can see the ball hitting your target, then you will hit that target. If you can see the ball going in the hole, then you will drain that putt. See victory, trust yourself, and prevail.

Now stay *in this moment* and enjoy it.

GUIDED VISUALIZATION: TENNIS

Imagine lying down in a park or the backyard on a quiet, sunny day. Feel the sun's heat on your forehead as all your tension melts away. The sunlight pours onto your eyelids, which become heavy with warmth. Sense the energy of the sunshine in your entire body. The sunlight rolls down your shoulders and through your back as it begins to relax. Breathe deeply. With every breath you are filled with light and warmth. In this stillness you are calm and comfortable. Enjoy this moment.

Now visualize yourself arriving at the tennis courts for an important tournament. This match means a lot because you are a competitor and it is time to play your best. Feeling powerful and unstoppable, be happy that you are a great player and destined to be a champion. Feel the satisfaction as the thousands of hours of practice take you to the here and now.

In the locker room or maybe the parking lot, as you change into your tennis shoes, you also change into a champion player. Walk to the courts and enjoy the crowd and the other players. Absorb the energy and excitement of competition. Smile at your friends and family. It is time to play.

Concentrate on each point and stay in the moment. The ball looks bigger and brighter today. Your stroke feels effortless. You are enjoying the simplicity of playing great tennis.

You see the ball clearly on your opponent's racquet and its return to your hitting zone—and you see it hit your sweet spot. At that nanosecond you remain balanced and focused on keeping your head still through the full stroke. The ball catapults off your racquet during your relaxed follow-through, and then you look up and move back into readiness. Your shot goes exactly as you envisioned and your opponent is scrambling.

Your mind is still: see, trust, do. As you watch your opponent's movements, you anticipate the next shot even before the ball has reached your opponent's racquet—there is no mental debate, just pure reaction. Of course, your opponent might hit a "ripper" and nick a line, which in no way means you were "wrong." Forget the judgmental "right or wrong" and accept that your opponent hit a great shot and is unlikely to do so consistently, especially against you.

Continue to place your shots strategically. A long rally does not bother you because the more you hit, the more you learn and the stronger you become. You prepare for the next shot, the next angle. The oldest cliché, to play one shot at a time, is the oldest for a reason: it is truth. Forget past matches and only remember how good it feels now—win or lose—as a superior player.

Know that you are strong physically, mentally, and emotionally—reining in the wild horses of doubt and fear. You know what you did to prepare. Could you have done more? Yes, if you had given up sleep and your sanity. You did what you could do and now accept that rest is as important as relentless practice. A rested mind is ready to let you be you.

You will miss a shot or two or more and will react to winners and unforced errors the same: point lost, next point the new goal. Each shot is the first shot of all matches. You are steadfastly committed to the simplicity of "see it, hit it," all day long.

Play free and loose and accept being yourself and playing your game. In between points follow your routine: towel off, breathe slowly, sip water, and stay in your *zone*. Only you can beat yourself, so do not help the opponent.

During a match, follow your game plan with the expectation that something good will happen. Whether you get a good or bad break, accept it. If your game plan appears to be failing, dump it and do not debate your decision. Play in the realm of trust. You know you are well prepared and destined to win often this year. Focus on how great your strokes feel, like the laser backhand down the line—and play tennis like you did as a kid playing a game, any game—be that kid. You have trained for this moment and now play this game. Simple? Yes. Let simplicity stay simple. It is only hard if you make it hard.

As you change sides during a match, think about your love of the game and reflect on your only goal: See it and hit it. What else matters? Accept that the simple answer is simply nothing.

On each shot, all you care about is getting the ball into your hitting zone and solidly striking it. Commit to each shot, hit through the ball with total trust in your preparation and your talent. Let the ball go where you want it to go—forcing is failing.

Each shot is a fresh shot. With patience and a quiet mind, you see the whole court and know your opponent. You already know that a consistent mental approach—shot by shot, all day, every day—lets your training let you win. The keys to winning are simple, unless you make them hard: one shot at a time, accept wherever the ball goes, find the ball, hit the ball—then repeat, repeat, repeat.

Your mind is silent as the ball nears your hitting zone. Trust your instincts and let it flow. Let the other players tighten up, take risky shots, and try to outguess you while you have fun. Settle down to the stillness that lets you see the seams on the ball, the spot where the ball bounces into your zone, and then hit it with solidity and purpose.

On the court, trust your instinct to see the ball and just hit it, as instinct is true every time and distrust often fails. A clear mind in the split-second moments easily reads where the ball is going as it leaves your opponent's racquet. Your training has sharpened your instincts. You relish your eagle eyes as the ball nears you and you react, trust, and perform.

Perhaps the match is long, with the outcome still uncertain. Your opponent starts to complain and get uptight. You stay happy, letting nothing change your mood. You are having fun doing whatever it takes to win. Eventually, your opponent makes a mistake, gets flustered, and quits. This does not bother or upset you, because you ignore it. This frustration gives you an edge.

At times the wind has swirled around the court. You decide you love the wind because you are a great athlete. Your mind is in control, not the conditions. Your mind focuses on getting closer to the ball and adjusting to crazy bounces. Let the elements bother the other player, not you.

Moments in the match have been ideal, and other moments were less so, but you love the game just the same. You stay out of your own way because of your calm, quiet mind. You spend the match just seeing the ball and hitting it. All day, all match, however long, it continues to be fun.

Love the challenge of accepting the simplicity of you, your opponent, and one ball. Nothing else matters. As you play better, you get calmer. With each well-placed shot, your mind becomes quieter. The more at ease you are, the more you enjoy the game.

Let the *zone* come to you. It will if you simply let your training, intuition, and athleticism take over. You are simply playing tennis. So be a player for the sheer joy of playing. You see clearly that tennis is a game to be played well by you.

Back in the match, you are serving to take the set. Everyone is watching and knows you need to hold for the win. You gather yourself and remember that your objective is the same as it was in the first game: See and hit your serve with a quiet mind. You already are a winner. If you stay focused on every shot, you will inevitably win your share of matches and tournaments. So, see the serve, toss the ball, hit it, and watch it bore through to the target.

You smile and feel satisfied as you run up to the net, shake hands, and accept congratulations. Enjoy accepting and hoisting the trophy. Listen to your family and friends cheering. All of this is enjoyable, but pause to notice how relaxed you were from the first serve to match point, how much fun you had, and how much trust you had in yourself.

You expect more days like this one, because you are going to keep tennis simple. Why? Because by having fun you just see and do, and then success happens. This is the best strategy for playing the game. Anything you can envision is possible and doable. If you can see the ball hitting your target, then you will hit that target. If you can see your shots nicking the lines, then you can hit them all day long. See victory, trust yourself, and prevail.

Now stay *in this moment* and enjoy it.

GUIDED VISUALIZATION: BASKETBALL

Close your eyes and start preparing for a game. Think about the details of the competition:

- Where is the competition?
- Who will be your opponents?
- How will they look?
- What is the color of their jerseys?
- Who will be in the stands?
- What do you want to accomplish with this mental practice?

Take your mind to game day. Begin your pregame routine. Notice your surroundings: sights, sounds, and people. As you're visualizing your surroundings, feel how you are in your own body and looking through your own eyes, listening through your own ears, and feeling the movement of your own body. You can feel the fabric of your uniform rub against your skin. Finally, clear your mind by putting any negative thoughts or fears in a virtual duffel bag and stuff it under the bench.

See yourself warming up and preparing to perform. Sink a few shots and go for some rebounds. Absorb the energy and excitement of competition. Hear the fans moving around. Soon, it will be time to compete!

Now, turn your attention to the correct execution of the techniques or skills associated with your sport. Watch yourself for a few moments performing solidly. See yourself sprinting up and down the court. Take a few passes and pass a few balls to teammates. Observe as you quickly take up good aggressive defense positions. Be in your body as you rebound and move for the next play. Shoot relaxed and see the ball falling through the net.

Notice the full focus that you have while competing. Then give yourself some challenging scenarios. See yourself making a mistake or responding to something that goes wrong. Quickly get back on defense after a turnover. Notice yourself making the proper adjustments to get *back on to your plays.* Trust yourself, love your game, and enjoy your feelings. Bring constant energy to both ends of the court. Be energized from start to finish.

Next, look around and see your teammates encouraging you and know that you support them, too. Listen to yourself being vocal on the court, *communicating* with your teammates (not just chatter or buzzing). Take in your surroundings and feel the energy. Continue to feel centered and in the *zone,* as you're a consistent shooter because there's just net touching your shots. Visualize some previous successful moments in a competition.

In this moment, you are in complete control of your body, your state of mind, and your overall performance. Feel a sense of confidence and control while fully executing your skills and techniques. Basketball is one of the most complex reactive sports, but you're wired right to play.

Visualize yourself going through a few more successful and happy scenarios. Give your teammate a good pass, move past a defender, zero in on the hoop (seems huge!). See, feel, and trust your training and your talent. Accept this truth: The better the competition and the more you are challenged, the more *enjoyable* the experience. There's nothing like sticking it to your competitors.

After moving through your challenges, return to a few more

typical competitive scenarios, executing them fluidly and without hesitation. Take a moment to notice everything around you:

- Your teammates are engaged in their roles and moving well to their positions.
- You feel connected to them and are supporting them as well.
- You can feed off or tune out the fans as needed.
- You feel that your body is strong and full of energy, and that you are mentally in the zone.

Run through a few more competitive scenarios as your preparation comes to an end. Feel the motion and pace of the game. After a few more positive scenes, prepare to finish the visualization. Good job. You are now at the end of the visualization exercise.

In the future, remember this feeling of physical and mental preparedness. After quiet reflection, start to feel yourself in your chair or bed. Feel yourself come back to your current surroundings. Focus your attention on your feet and wiggle your toes and flex your ankles. Then open and close your hands, stretch out your arms. Sit up straight and take a few deep breaths. Open your eyes and engage all your senses. Let yourself focus on the sounds around you. Feel your skin tingle. Feel the energy in your body. Let your surroundings come into focus. Good job.

Now stay *in this moment* and enjoy it.

GUIDED VISUALIZATION: SOCCER

Close your eyes and start preparing for a game. Think about the details of the soccer game:

- Where is the competition?

- Who will be your opponents?

- How will they look?

- What is the color of their jerseys?

- What is the weather like?

- Who will be in the stands?

- What do you want to accomplish with this mental practice?

Take your mind to the competition. Begin your precompetition routines. That's right. Notice your surroundings: sights, sounds, and people. See the field stretching out in front of you. See the blue sky above and the green grass below. As you're visualizing your surroundings, feel how you are in your own body and looking through your own eyes, listening through your own ears, and feeling the movement of your own body. You can feel the fabric of your uniform rub against your skin. The grass crunches under your cleats. Finally, clear your mind by putting any negative thoughts or fears in a virtual duffel bag and stuff it under the bench.

See yourself warming up properly and preparing to perform. Do a few sprints up and down the field. Your body comes alive. Absorb the energy and excitement of competition. Soon, it will be time to compete!

Now, turn your attention to the correct execution of the techniques or skills associated with your sport. Watch yourself for a few moments performing solidly. Move the ball solidly upfield, get back quickly for defense, and run through some patterns. Notice the full focus that you have while competing. Give yourself some challenging scenarios. See yourself making a mistake or responding to something that goes wrong. Get back into a play quickly, and make some good passes after avoiding defenders. Notice yourself making the proper adjustments to get *back into your position* and *focused on executing plays.* Just trust yourself, love your game, and enjoy your feelings. Excellent!

If you are a goalie, be alert and see the ball well. Get big and challenge the shooter. Block the shot and control the ball. Stay cool and calm.

Next, look around and see your teammates encouraging you and know that you support them, too. Hear their words and yourself talking as plays develop. Take in your surroundings and feel the energy. Continue to feel centered and in the *zone.* Visualize some additional successful moments in the competition.

In this moment, you are in complete control of your body, your state of mind, and your overall performance. Feel a sense of confidence and control while fully executing your skills and techniques.

Visualize yourself going through a few more successful and happy scenarios. See, feel, and trust your training and talent Accept this truth: The better the competition and the more you are challenged, the more *enjoyable* the experience.

After moving through your challenges, return to a few more typical competitive scenarios, executing them fluidly and without hesitation. Take a moment to notice everything around you:

• Your teammates are engaged in their roles or perhaps cheering you on.

• You feel connected to them and are supporting them as well.

• You can feed off or tune out the fans as needed.

• You feel that your body is strong and full of energy, and that you are mentally in the *zone.*

Run through a few more competitive scenarios that will apply to this match. Feel the motion and pace of the competition. As your heart races in the match scenarios, prepare to wind things down. Kick a few more balls into the goal and finish. Good job. You are now at the end of the visualization exercise.

In the future, remember this feeling of physical and mental preparedness. After quiet reflection, start to feel yourself in your chair or bed. Feel yourself come back to your current surroundings. Focus your attention on your feet and wiggle your toes and flex your ankles. Then open and close your hands and stretch out your arms. Sit up straight and take a few deep breaths. Open your eyes and engage all your senses. Let yourself focus on the sounds around you. Feel your skin tingle. Feel the energy in your body. Let your surroundings come into focus. Good job.

Now stay *in this moment* and enjoy it.

GUIDED VISUALIZATION: VOLLEYBALL

Close your eyes and start preparing for a competition. Think about the details of the expected volleyball matchup:

- Where is the competition?
- Who will be your opponents?
- How will they look?
- What is the color of their jerseys?
- Who will be in the stands?
- What do you want to accomplish with this mental practice?

Take your mind to the competition. Begin your precompetition routines. That's right. Notice your surroundings, whether they are sights, sounds, and people. How does the gym look? Bright lights or windows? As you're visualizing your surroundings, feel how you are in your own body and looking through your own eyes, listening through your own ears, and feeling the movement of your own body. You can feel the fabric of your uniform rub against your skin. Finally, clear your mind by putting any negative thoughts or fears in a virtual duffel bag and stuff it under the bench.

See yourself warming up properly and preparing to perform. Go through your stretch routine and then move the ball around with your teammates. Absorb the energy and excitement of competition. Go through your warm-up routine for blocking, loading, and exploding into shots. See your hands clearly lining up and timing hits perfectly. Soon, it will be time to compete!

Now, turn your attention to the correct execution of the techniques or skills associated with your sport. Watch yourself for a few moments performing solidly. Notice the full focus that you have while competing. Feel a good rhythm during your service routine. Give yourself some challenging scenarios. For setting, square up and set the ball at a perfect height for your teammate. Be vocal on the court, communicate, and encourage your teammates. Then see yourself make a mistake or respond to something that goes wrong. Dig for a few balls, predicting where the ball will go. Then notice yourself making the proper adjustments to get *back on the right track*. Trust yourself, love your game, and enjoy your feelings. Good job!

Next, look around and see your teammates encouraging you and know that you support them, too. This is a team sport and this is the best team! Take in your surroundings and feel the energy. Feel light and powerful, confident and energized. Continue to feel centered and in the *zone*. Visualize some prior successful moments in the competition.

In this moment, you are in complete control of your body, state of mind, and overall performance. Feel a sense of confidence and control while fully executing your skills and techniques. Notice how everything has slowed down. You are a magnet for the ball, and you can put the ball where you want. This is the *zone*.

Visualize yourself going through a few more successful scenarios. See, feel, and trust your training and talent Accept this truth: The better the competition and the more you are challenged, the more *enjoyable* the experience. Go for your shots and hit your spots.

After moving through your challenges, return to a few more typical competitive scenarios, executing them fluidly and without hesitation. Take a moment to notice everything around you:

• Your teammates are engaged in their roles or perhaps cheering you on.

• You feel connected to them and are supporting them as well by coming together after each point.

• You can feed off or tune out the fans as needed.

• You feel that your body is strong, full of energy, and you are mentally in the *zone*.

Run through a few more competitive scenarios as your preparation comes to an end. Feel the motion and pace of the match peak, and then get ready to get off the court. Good job. You are now at the end of the visualization exercise.

In the future, remember this feeling of physical and mental preparedness. After quiet reflection, start to feel yourself in your chair or bed. Feel yourself come back to your current surroundings. Focus your attention on your feet and wiggle your toes and flex your ankles. Then open and close your hands, stretch out your arms. Sit up straight and take a few deep breaths. Open your eyes and engage all your senses. Let yourself focus on the sounds around you. Feel your skin tingle. Feel the energy in your body. Let your surroundings come into focus. Good job.

Now stay *in this moment* and enjoy it.

GUIDED VISUALIZATION: CROSS-COUNTRY

Visualize arriving early at the starting area. Spectators and competitors are moving about. Signs and barricades divide the spectators from the athletes. You look around to orient yourself. You are about to run 3.1 miles, stride by stride.

This event means a lot to you. Feeling totally powerful and unstoppable, you know it's now time to race your best. You're happy about the training you've put in and satisfied with your training. All your efforts have made the here and now—*now.*

Your calm pre-race mind-set transforms into the focused mind-set of an elite runner. Walk to the starting area and enjoy the bustling of the crowd and the energy surrounding the other runners. Absorb the energy and excitement of impending competition. Smile at your friends and family. See the flags in front of the starting area and see the starting line—it's time to run. You're primed and destined to race your best.

Concentrate on this race—*stay in the moment.* Enter your mental starting gate, narrow your focus, and expand your breathing. React to the starting gun without thinking and let motion flow into your body—a steady start followed by relaxed and well-paced strides. Your pre-race plan is now an in-race plan. You shed all negativity and discomfort with one stride, the first stride. Maintain an easy pace, knowing that you started strong and can finish stronger.

"Take one mile at a time" is a cliché for a good reason: it's true. Forget past times and personal bests and only remember how good it feels *now* to be running strong. Each mile is the first mile of a new race (three in a row, and then just a bit more). Be committed to the simplicity of "see, trust, run"—all race long. Run free and smooth and accept that you can only race *your* race. Commit to each mile, run within yourself, let your steady strides carry you along, and trust in your training, talent, and mind.

No other runners can pressure you. Just forget them and enjoy the simplicity of running smoothly. Allow your body to do what you've trained it to do. Know that you're strong physically, mentally, and emotionally. You are out-running the two imposters: doubt and discomfort. You have prepared well. Accept that you have what it takes *right now*.

Stay on course and expect something good to happen. If you hit a good and/or bad running patch, accept the good one or both equally. You are well-prepared to handle anything. Bring up a few challenges. The steep incline ahead will be a test and the most difficult part of the course. You have prepared for this, and welcome the effort. Focus on how great your strides feel and then run fearlessly like you did as a kid—*be that kid*. You have trained for this moment, so now run *in the moment*. Simple? Should be. Let simplicity stay simple. Do not make hard what need not be hard.

Each mile is your first mile, and with confidence and a *quiet mind*, you're going to go farther. You already know that a consistent mental approach—stride by stride, all day, every mile—lets your training guide you to success. The keys to performing your best are simple, unless you make them hard, and you won't. Say to yourself: one mile at a time, run like a champion, accept what happens—then repeat, repeat, repeat.

As you run, at times the surrounding noise and haste may distract you. When you feel any distraction, tone down the crowd, dwell in your own world, and follow your race plan. Instinct is what drives you now, so let it *flow*. While other runners tighten up, pace poorly at the beginning, and hit the wall before the end—you're having *fun*. Stay in your own inner stillness, which lets you find your easy speed, stride by stride, and find the finish in your own time. For your own victory.

You may encounter unexpected race conditions, and other runners may falter, complain, and get uptight. Silence them in your mind and stay in your *zone*. Having fun is the prelude to having your best performance. Your mind is in control, not the clock or conditions. A still and quiet mind is your racer's edge.

Love the challenge of accepting the simplicity of your running, path, and purpose. Nothing else matters. As you run farther, you'll get calmer. As each well-executed mile passes, let it go and enjoy the next stride.

As you pass the halfway mark, let the *zone* come to you as you keep it simple by letting your training, intuition, and athleticism take over. You're running, which is a form of playing. So be a runner for the sheer joy of running.

Now, your final stretch approaches. Tell yourself that your final racing goal is the same as your first racing goal: trust and a quiet mind. You're already a winner. If you stay focused within every mile, then you will inevitably perform your best. See it, feel it, and trust it as you run smoothly across and beyond the finish line. Slow after crossing the line.

As a sense of accomplishment floods over you. Smile and give high fives to other runners. Listen to family and friends cheering. All of this is enjoyable, so pause to absorb how relaxed you were from the start to the finish, how much fun you had, and that you trusted yourself.

Then expect more races like this one, because you're going to keep running *simple*. Why? Because having fun is seeing and running and letting excellence happen. Anything you can envision is possible and doable. If you can see the best times, then you'll get the best times. See success, trust yourself, and prevail.

Now slowly take in a couple of deep breaths. Wiggle your toes and your fingers. Shake out your legs. As you breathe in, open your eyes and refocus. Take another deep breath. Now stay *in this moment* and enjoy it.

GUIDED VISUALIZATION:
CYCLING

Visualize arriving early at the bike starting area, which may still be dark in the morning light. Spectators and competitors are moving about. Other athletes are prepping and checking equipment. Signs and barricades divide the spectators from the athletes. You look around to orient yourself. You are about to start.

This event means a lot to you. Feeling totally powerful and unstoppable, you know it's now time to race your best. You're happy about the training you've put in and satisfied with it. You've put in the miles, mile after mile. All your efforts have made the here and now—*now.*

Your calm pre-race mind-set transforms into the focused mind-set of an elite cyclist. Move to the starting area and enjoy the bustling of the crowd and the energy surrounding the other competitors. Absorb the energy and excitement of impending competition. Smile at your friends and family. See the flags in front of the starting area and see the starting line—it's time to pedal. You're primed and destined to race your best.

Concentrate on this race—stay *in the moment.* Enter your mental starting gate, narrow your focus, and expand your breathing. React to the starting gun without thinking and let motion flow into your body and bike—a steady start followed by relaxed and well-paced revolutions. Your pre-race plan is now an in-race plan. You shed all negativity and discomfort as the wind hits your face. Maintain an easy pace, knowing that you started strong and will finish stronger.

"Take one mile at a time" is a cliché for a good reason: it's true. Forget past times and personal bests and only remember how good it feels *now* to be biking strong. Each mile is the first mile of a new course. Be committed to the simplicity—all race long. Cycle free and smoothly and accept that you can only race *your* race.

Commit to each mile, and stay within yourself, let your steady pace carry you along, and trust in your training, talent, and mind.

No other cyclists can pressure you. If they go for a sprint, follow your game plan. Either join the pursuit or forget them and enjoy executing your plan. Allow your body to do what you've trained it to do. Know that you're strong physically, mentally, and emotionally. You are outmaneuvering the two imposters: doubt and discomfort. You have prepared. Accept that you have what it takes *right now*.

Stay on course and expect something good to happen. If a good and/or bad patch emerges, accept the good one or both equally. You are well-prepared to handle anything. Stay hydrated and return to your nutrition plan as needed. Focus on how great your bike feels and move fearlessly in the wind like you did as a kid—*be that kid*. You have trained for this moment, so now stay *in the moment*. Simple? Should be. Let simplicity stay simple. Do not make hard what need not be hard. Don't do it.

Each mile is your first mile, and with confidence and a *quiet mind*, you're going to go farther. You already know that a consistent mental approach—with a steady pace, all day, every mile—lets your training guide you to success. The keys to performing your best are simple, unless you make them hard and you won't. Say to yourself: one mile at a time, flow like a champion, accept what happens—then repeat, repeat, repeat.

As you cycle past key spots, at times the surrounding noise and haste may distract you. When you feel any distraction, tone down the crowd, dwell in your own world, and follow your race plan. Instinct is what drives you now, so let it *flow*. While other cyclists tighten up, pace poorly at the beginning, and hit the wall before the end—you're having *fun*. Stay in your own inner stillness, which lets you find your easy speed, rhythm, and cross the finish in your own time, for your own victory.

You may encounter unexpected race conditions, and other cyclists may falter, complain, and get uptight. Silence them in your mind and stay in your *zone*. Having fun is the prelude to having your best performance. Your mind is in control, not the clock or conditions. A still and quiet mind is your racer's edge.

Love the challenge of accepting the simplicity of your biking, your path, and your purpose. Nothing else matters. As you go farther, you'll get calmer. As each well-executed mile passes, let it go and enjoy the next curve or straightaway.

As you hit important course markers, let the *zone* come to you as you keep it simple by letting your training, intuition, and athleticism take over. You're biking, which is a form of playing and really just moving from point A to point B. So cycle for the sheer joy of moving through the wind.

Now, your final stretch approaches. Tell yourself that your final racing goal is the same as your first racing goal: trust and a quiet mind. You're already a winner. If you stay focused within every mile, then you will inevitably perform your best. See it, feel it, and trust it as you pedal smoothly across the finish line.

As a sense of accomplishment floods over you. Smile and give high fives to other cyclists. Listen to family and friends cheering. All of this is enjoyable, so pause to absorb how relaxed you were from the start to the finish, how much fun you had, and that you trusted yourself.

Then expect more races like this one, because you're going to keep biking simple. Why? Because having fun is doing and biking and letting excellence happen. Anything you can envision is possible and doable. If you can see the best times, then you'll get the best times. See success, trust yourself, and prevail.

Now slowly take in a couple of deep breaths. Wiggle your toes and your fingers. Shake out your legs. As you breathe in, open your eyes and refocus. Take another deep breath. Now stay *in this moment* and enjoy it.

GUIDED VISUALIZATION: HOCKEY

Close your eyes and start preparing for a game. Think about the details of the hockey game:

- Where is the competition?
- Who will be your opponent?
- How will they look?
- What is the color of their jerseys?
- Who will be in the crowd?
- What do you want to accomplish with this mental practice?

Take your mind to game day. Begin your pregame routine. Breathe in the cold air as you step on the ice. Notice your surroundings: sights, sounds, and people. As you're visualizing your surroundings, feel how you are in your own body and looking through your own eyes, listening through your own ears, and feeling the movement of your own body. You can feel the fabric of your uniform rub against your skin. Finally, clear your mind by putting any negative thoughts or fears in a virtual duffel bag and stuff it under the bench.

See yourself warming up and preparing to perform. Skate a couple laps and take some shots on goal. Work on your stick handling. Absorb the energy and excitement of competition. Hear the fans moving around. Soon, it will be time to compete!

Now, turn your attention to the correct execution of the techniques or skills associated with your sport. Watch yourself for a few moments performing solidly. See yourself skating up and down the ice. Go for a loose puck. Shoot relaxed and see the puck tickle the twine.

If you are a goalie, be alert and see the puck well. Get big and challenge the shooter. Block the shot and control the puck. Stay cool and calm.

Notice the full focus that you have while competing. Then give yourself some challenging scenarios. See yourself making a mistake or responding to something that goes wrong. Make the proper adjustments. Drive the net. Move your feet. Track back hard. Trust yourself, love your game, and enjoy your feelings. Bring constant energy to all zones. Attack from start to finish. Get stronger with each shift.

Next, look around and see your teammates encouraging you and know that you support them, too. Listen to yourself being vocal on the ice, *communicating* with your teammates (not just chatter or buzzing). Take in your surroundings and feel the energy. Continue to feel centered and in the *zone*.

In this moment, you are in complete control of your body, state of mind, and overall performance. Feel a sense of confidence and control while fully executing your skills and techniques. Win the battle. Push the pace. Hockey is one of the most complex reactive sports, but you're wired right to play.

Visualize yourself going through a few more successful scenarios. Give your teammate a good pass, move past a defender, zero in on the net (seems huge!). See, feel, and trust your training and talent. Accept this truth: The better the competition and the more you are challenged, the more you will *enjoy* the experience. There's nothing like sticking it to your competitors—as that's what they're trying to do to you.

After moving through your challenges, return to a few more typical competitive scenarios, executing them fluidly and without hesitation. Take a moment to notice everything around you:

• Your teammates are engaged in their roles and moving well to their positions.

• You feel connected to them and are supporting them as well.

• You can feed off or tune out the fans as needed.

• You feel that your body is strong and full of energy, and you are mentally in the *zone*.

Run through a few more competitive scenarios as your preparation comes to an end. Feel the motion and pace of the game. After a few more positive scenes, prepare to finish the visualization. Good job. You are now at the end of the visualization exercise.

In the future, remember this feeling of physical and mental preparedness. After quiet reflection, start to feel yourself in your chair or bed. Feel yourself come back to your current surroundings. Focus your attention on your feet and wiggle your toes and flex your ankles. Then open and close your hands, stretch out your arms. Sit up straight and take a few deep breaths. Open your eyes and engage all your senses. Let yourself focus on the sounds around you. Feel your skin tingle. Feel the energy in your body. Let your surroundings come into focus. Good job.

Now stay *in this moment* and enjoy it.

GUIDED VISUALIZATION: BASEBALL/SOFTBALL

Close your eyes and start preparing for a game. Think about the details of the competition:

• Where is the competition?

• Who will be your opponent?

• How will they look?

- What is the color of their jerseys?

- Who will be in the stands?

- What do you want to accomplish with this mental practice?

Take your mind to game day. Begin your pregame routine. Breathe in the fresh air as you step on the field. Notice your surroundings: sights, sounds, and people. As you're visualizing your surroundings, feel how you are in your own body and looking through your own eyes, listening through your own ears, and feeling the movement of your own body. You can feel the fabric of your uniform rub against your skin. Finally, clear your mind by putting any negative thoughts or fears in a virtual duffel bag and stuff it under the bench.

See yourself warming up and preparing to compete. Execute your pregame routine. See and feel yourself stretching and then playing catch. Absorb the energy and excitement of competition. Hear the fans moving around. Soon, it will be time to compete!

Now, turn your attention to the correct execution of the techniques or skills associated with your position. Watch yourself for a few moments performing solidly. See yourself doing what you do best.

Notice the full focus that you have while competing. Then give yourself some challenging scenarios. Respond like a champion to anything that goes wrong. Quickly regroup after a poor pitch or an error in the field. Take a deep breath and command yourself to "forget it." You are a master of letting go and staying positive. Notice yourself making the proper adjustments to get *back into a winning mind-set*. Trust yourself, love your game, and enjoy your feelings. In short, play happy. Bring constant energy for every pitch. You are always focused on this pitch at this moment.

Next, look around and see your teammates encouraging you and know that you support them, too. Listen to yourself being vocal on the field, *communicating* with your teammates (not just chatter or buzzing). Take in your surroundings and feel the energy. Continue to feel centered and in the *zone,* as you're a solid player because every play is yours to make. Visualize some previous successful moments in a competition. Smile often, as it will make your opponents wonder what you're thinking.

In this moment, you are in complete control of your body, your state of mind, and your overall performance. Feel a sense of confidence and control while fully executing your skills and strategies. Baseball is one of the most complex reactive sports, but you're wired right to play.

Visualize yourself going through a few more successful and happy scenarios. For batters: see the ball as big, take good balanced swings, and hit line drives up the middle. On defense, you want the ball hit to you. You get a good first step and make a play.

For pitchers: You maintain a confident mound presence, no matter what happens. Give the batter credit for getting a hit. Then move on to the next batter. See, feel, and trust your training and your talent. Pound the strike zone. Every pitch is yours to win. Accept this truth: The better the competition and the more you are challenged, the more *enjoyable* the experience. There's nothing like sticking it to your competitors—as that's what they're trying to do to you.

Move through a few more competitive scenarios, executing them fluidly and without hesitation. Take a moment to notice everything around you:

• Your teammates are engaged in their roles and moving well to their positions.

• You feel connected to them and are supporting them as well.

• You can feed off or tune out the fans as needed.

- You feel that your body is strong and full of energy, and that you are mentally in the *zone.*

You have infinite patience because you have a calm mind. You already know that a consistent mental approach—pitch by pitch, every inning all game—allows your training to let you win. The keys to competing are simple, so don't make them hard: one pitch at a time, flow with the swing, catch or throw, accept the results, then repeat, repeat, repeat.

Run through a few more competitive scenarios as your preparation comes to an end. Breathe easily and deeply. Feel the motion and pace of the game slow down. After a few more positive scenes, prepare to finish the visualization. Good job. You are now at the end of the visualization exercise.

In the future, remember this feeling of physical and mental preparedness. After quiet reflection, start to feel yourself in your chair or bed. Feel yourself come back to your current surroundings. Focus your attention on your feet and wiggle your toes and flex your ankles. Then open and close your hands, stretch out your arms. Sit up straight and take a few deep breaths. Open your eyes and engage all your senses. Let yourself focus on the sounds around you. Feel your skin tingle. Feel the energy in your body. Let your surroundings come into focus. Good job.

Now stay *in this moment* and enjoy it.

GUIDED VISUALIZATION: AMERICAN FOOTBALL

Close your eyes and start preparing for a game. Think about the details of the competition:

- Where is the competition?
- Who will be your opponent?
- How will they look?
- What is the color of their jerseys?
- Who will be in the stands?
- What do you want to accomplish with this mental practice?

Take your mind to game day. Begin your pregame routine. Breathe in the fresh air as you step on the gridiron. Notice your surroundings: sights, sounds, and people. As you're visualizing your surroundings, feel how you are in your own body and looking through your own eyes, listening through your own ears, and feeling the movement of your own body. You can feel the fabric of your uniform rub against your skin. Finally, clear your mind by putting any negative thoughts or fears in a virtual duffel bag and stuff it under the bench.

See yourself warming up and preparing to compete. Execute your pregame routine. See and feel yourself stretching and then playing catch. Absorb the energy and excitement of competition. Hear the fans moving around. Soon, it will be time to compete!

Now, turn your attention to the correct execution of the techniques or skills associated with your position. Watch yourself for a few moments performing solidly. See yourself doing what you do best.

Notice the full focus that you have while competing. Then give yourself some challenging scenarios. Respond like a champion to anything that goes wrong. Quickly regroup after a poor play or a fumble on the field. Take a deep breath and command yourself to "forget it." You are a master of letting go and staying positive. Notice yourself making the proper adjustments to get *back into your winning mind-set.* Trust yourself, love your game, and enjoy your feelings. In short, compete with joy. Bring constant energy for every down. You are always focused on this play at this moment.

Next, look around and see your teammates encouraging you and know that you support them, too. Listen to yourself being vocal on the field, *communicating* with your teammates (not just chatter or buzzing). Take in your surroundings and feel the energy. Continue to feel centered and in the *zone,* as you're a solid player because every play is yours to make. Visualize some previous successful moments in a competition.

In this moment, you are in complete control of your body, your state of mind, and your overall performance. Feel a sense of confidence and control while fully executing your skills and strategies. Football is one of the most complex reactive sports, but you're wired right to play.

Visualize yourself going through a few more successful and positive scenarios. For quarterbacks: You have good field vision and a strong arm. Work through your progressions and make the play. For running backs: Picture yourself eluding defenders or knocking them over like a bowling ball. For receivers, you are a good route runner with quick feet and good hands. Run a few routes and score some touchdowns. Your run-after-the-catch skills are strong.

For defensive players: Aggressively swarm the ball. Picture yourself making tackles, sacks, and interceptions. You are a superb pass rusher and you close on the quarterback in a hurry. See, feel, and trust your training and your talent. Accept this truth: The better the competition and the more you are challenged, the more *enjoyable* the experience. There's nothing like sticking it to your competitors—as that's what they're trying to do to you.

Move through a few more competitive scenarios, executing

them fluidly and without hesitation. Take a moment to notice everything around you:

- Your teammates are engaged in their roles and moving well to their positions.
- You feel connected to them and are supporting them as well.
- You can feed off or tune out the fans as needed.
- You feel that your body is strong, full of energy, and you are mentally in the *zone*.

You have infinite patience because you have a calm mind. You already know that a consistent mental approach—down by down, every drive all game—allows your training to let you win. The keys to competing are simple, so don't make them hard: one play at a time, flow with the tackle, catch or throw, accept the results, then repeat, repeat, repeat.

Run through a few more competitive scenarios as your preparation comes to an end. Breathe easily and deeply. Feel the motion and pace of the game slow down. After a few more positive scenes, prepare to finish the visualization. Good job. You are now at the end of the visualization exercise.

In the future, remember this feeling of physical and mental preparedness. After quiet reflection, start to feel yourself in your chair or bed. Feel yourself come back to your current surroundings. Focus your attention on your feet and wiggle your toes and flex your ankles. Then open and close your hands, stretch out your arms. Sit up straight and take a few deep breaths. Open your eyes and engage all your senses. Let yourself focus on the sounds around you. Feel your skin tingle. Feel the energy in your body. Let your surroundings come into focus. Good job.

Now stay *in this moment* and enjoy it.

GUIDED VISUALIZATION: GYMNASTICS

Close your eyes and start preparing for a gymnastics meet. Think about the details of the competition:

- Where is the competition?
- Who will you be competing against?
- Who will be the judges?
- What competition leotard will you be wearing?
- What do you want to accomplish with this mental practice?

Be sensory:

- Walk into the competition site
- Smell the popcorn and other spectator foods
- Feel the fabric of your leotard rub against your skin
- See the crowd
- Feel the floor and stand in line
- Hear your name and acknowledge the summons

Now, go to your first event area and warm up. Feel the dry, rough chalk on your hands and feet. Taste a sip of the cold sports drink before and after your warmup.

For the vault, your keywords are *run fast, strong arms, punch the board, arms up, drive the heels,* and *stick the landing.* Now, execute your vault. Feel strong and energized. Smile as you stick the landing. Hear the crowd clapping. Feel the sense of satisfaction of nailing your goal score.

Move on, executing your beam, bar, and floor routines, one at a time. Trust your training by letting your body do what you have trained it to do. Compete with purpose, passion, and a fearless mind-set.

Keep things simple, stay in the moment, and respond to everything with total acceptance. Can you stumble on a skill and still continue with confidence? Of course you can. Don't get upset, frustrated, or flustered.

Be tension free, stay in rhythm, you underreact to anything negative.

In this moment, you are in complete control of your body, your state of mind, and your overall performance. Feel a sense of confidence and control while fully executing your skills and techniques. Gymnastics is one of the most complex sports, but you're wired right to perform.

Visualize yourself going through a few more successful and happy scenarios. See, feel, and trust your training and your talent. Accept this truth: The better the competition and the more you are challenged, the more *enjoyable* the experience. After moving through your challenges, return to a few more typical competitive scenarios, executing them fluidly and without hesitation.

After a few more positive scenes, prepare to finish the visualization. Fast-forward to the end of the meet. Stand tall and proud on the award stand. Feel that feeling of accomplishment and know that you achieved your goal score for each event.

Good job. You are now at the end of the visualization exercise.

In the future, remember this feeling of physical and mental preparedness. After quiet reflection, start to feel yourself in your chair or bed. Feel yourself come back to your current surroundings. Focus your attention on your feet and wiggle your toes and flex your ankles. Then open and close your hands, stretch out your arms. Sit up straight and take a few deep breaths. Open your eyes and engage all your senses. Let yourself focus on the sounds around you. Feel your skin tingle. Feel the energy in your body. Let your surroundings come into focus. Good job.

Now stay *in this moment* and enjoy it.

FINISH LINE

In sum, all champions have learned to visualize. They can see, early on, their success in their own mind, long before it actually comes about in the real world. They feel their performance in their body, and they have learned to trust their talent in competition.

A very important part of their preparation includes mental training—specifically, going through visualization. Utilize the examples given here, or adapt them to be unique for you. For additional guided-imagery scripts in other sports, check out *The Champion's Comeback*, which also includes scripts for a comeback visualization exercise, an academics visualization exercise, a fitness visualization exercise, and an injury-recovery visualization exercise.

See it, believe it, do it.

CHAPTER SIX

PERSONAL RESPONSIBILITY— MY ZONE OF CONTROL

**Work on yourself first, take responsibility
for your own progress.**

—THE I CHING

hen you're paying attention, things go better. No one knows what you are doing better than you! So this chapter focuses on four key areas that are often neglected by teens. These areas are highlighted to build a comprehensive and solid approach to your academic and athletic excellence. Take personal responsibility for each and for what is in your zone of control. We talked with several experts in these areas to provide specifics and actionable items, and to point you in the right direction:

• Sports Counseling

• Sleep Science

• Social Media

• Sports Nutrition

SPORTS COUNSELING

Ask for help. Not because you are weak.
But because you want to remain strong.

—LES BROWN

Mike Mombrea is the Employee Assistance Program Director for the San Francisco Giants, a licensed marriage and family therapist, and a certified employee assistance professional. Mike was formerly director of Adolescent and Family Programs at Youth and Family Services in Solano County, California, and EAP counselor at Cisco Systems Integrated Healthcare Center in San Jose, California. Here's Mike's advice for student-athletes.

1. It takes courage to admit when you're struggling and to ask for help. Greatness doesn't come from doing it alone. You get better faster when you use the resources available to you. Ask any true champion!

2. Train yourself to have a calm mind by practicing the following exercise every day. Set the alarm on your smartphone five minutes ahead, close your eyes, focus on your breath, and let distracting thoughts pass until the alarm goes off. Feel the difference. You can do this exercise between classes, before practice or at night before sleep. During competition, take a few "clearing breaths" to focus on the present moment and then let it rip.

3. Negative thoughts will occur from time to time. When you notice them, you are not failing. View negative thoughts (e.g., "I'm not good at this") like clouds passing in the sky. Take a "clearing breath," and reset to a positive intention ("I can do this!"). This process of switching to positivity takes time and repetition.

4. When it is time to compete, a key understanding is to know that you can work with whatever state of mind or mood you are in rather than getting in your head about not being or feeling 100 percent. The goal is to be the best that you can be every day.

5. Do not allow what anyone else is doing around you (critics, opponents, officials) to impact your approach or get in the way of your talent. Once you realize that what is going on around you can never be an excuse for poor performance, you'll be able to focus on your game 100 percent. What others are doing is outside your control and always will be. Make peace with this fact.

6. Being the best you can be and striving for excellence on and off the field is the aim. Others (opponents, spectators, and even negative teammates) may not like you, but your approach and commitment will command their respect. At the end of the day, you must live with you, not them. The sky is the limit when you're confident in yourself.

7. Support your teammates, it's good for your soul. Helping your teammates to have a great practice or competition will help you steer clear of negative thinking. We often put too much pressure on our own personal performance. In fact, the more you emphasize being a team player, the better you'll become as an individual player.

Snapshot: Be courageous enough to ask for help when you need it. Let negative thoughts come—and go! Learn how to maintain your composure, and ignore what you can't control. Lastly, be a team player; this will make the best parts of you even better. So go for a basketball-like triple double in points, total rebounds, assists, steals, or blocks! Be a complete person and champion.

SLEEP SCIENCE

Fatigue makes cowards of us all.

—VINCE LOMBARDI

Cheri D. Mah, MS, is a clinical and translational research fellow at the University of California San Francisco (UCSF) Human Performance Center and UCSF School of Medicine. Her research focuses on the relationship between sleep and performance in elite athletes.

Cheri consults on optimal performance and recovery strategies with professional teams, such as the world champion Golden State Warriors (NBA), San Francisco Giants (MLB), San Jose Sharks (NHL), Pittsburgh Steelers (NFL), Toronto Blue Jays, and teams in the NFL, NBA, NHL, and MLB. Currently an advisor on sleep for the Nike Performance Council, Cheri has developed comprehensive sleep programs for professional and collegiate sports. She advises varsity teams at Stanford on optimal sleep, scheduling, and peak performance. These programs integrate sleep education, technology, and applied sleep research to optimize performance and recovery.

Cheri shared with me eight key suggestions for how student-athletes can master their sleep. In addition, she provides two sleep and recovery goals, as well as online resources for additional information.

1. Reduce/eliminate caffeine. Refrain from caffeine (coffee, tea, energy drinks) in the late afternoon and early evening.

2. Be strategic with hydration and try a presleep snack. Consider a complex carbohydrate + protein snack before bed (e.g., cereal + milk). Prioritize good hydration during the day and reduce liquids one hour before bed.

3. Make your bedroom like a cave—dark, quiet, cool, and comfortable. Blackout curtains are strongly recommended, or use an eye mask. Earplugs can minimize noise and a fan circulates air while doubling as a white-noise machine. Cooler temperatures are better for sleep quality (60 to 67 degrees).

4. Power down. Make your bedroom a technology-free zone and eliminate distractions.

5. Prioritize a 20- to 30-minute routine (e.g., reading, stretching, yoga) before bed to prepare your body to sleep. Avoid TV, laptop, and video games one hour before bed. The bright light from these devices can prevent sleep and decrease melatonin release. Melatonin regulates our sleep cycles.

6. Establish a consistent sleep schedule. Go to bed and wake up at the same time every day. Set a daily alarm on your phone to remind you that you have 30 minutes to wrap up your day and head to bed.

7. Obtain 8 to10 hours of sleep every night. Adequate sleep is critical every day, not just the night before a game.

8. Leverage 20 to 30 minutes power nap/pregame nap. Power naps provide a temporary boost in alertness and performance, but are not a replacement for adequate sleep at night. Be cautious of longer naps, which can result in sleep inertia (feelings of sluggishness) upon awakening from deep stages of sleep.

SLEEP AND RECOVERY GOALS

1. Pay back accumulated sleep debt (accumulates from chronic inadequate sleep) and prioritize sleep over the entire season, not just the night before a game.

2. Aim for 8 to10 hours of sleep every night. Start by adding 30 minutes (e.g., go from 7 to 7.5 hours).

ONLINE RESOURCES

1. National Sleep Foundation—sleepfoundation.org

2. American Academy of Sleep Medicine—aasmnet.org

Snapshot: After a busy day, every day, take time to wind down and prepare for sleep. This is just as important as warming up before a match, practicing your fundamentals, or staying positive. Your body uses sleep to recover, clear toxins, build muscle, and solidify neural patterns. In other words, you need a good dose of sleep to be at your best!

SOCIAL MEDIA

It takes 20 years to build a reputation and 5 minutes to ruin it. If you think about that, you'll do things differently.

—WARREN BUFFETT

Joan Ryan is an award-winning journalist and author. She has written four books, including *Little Girls in Pretty Boxes: The Making and Breaking of Elite Gymnasts and Figure Skaters* (1995, Doubleday), which *Sports Illustrated* named one of the Top 100 Sports Books of All Time. She is also the media consultant for the San Francisco Giants. You don't have to be a teen to benefit from her advice about contemporary society.

Social media is like a torch: It can illuminate or incinerate.

Coaches, teammates, fans, college admissions staff, and

employers will form an impression of you through social media long before they meet you. Every comment and photo you post—or have ever posted—tells them what kind of person you are. Even your retweets become part of the picture. You post it, you own it.

So, as an athlete, you need a strategy. Here's a way to start. Think of three character traits you want people to know about you. (Examples might be loyalty, intelligence, selflessness, perseverance, focus, humor, and enthusiasm.) Make a note of them in your phone or on a piece of paper. In everything you post on social media and in everything you say to reporters, you need to project those qualities. Put another way, you can either leave it to chance that people will figure out who you are and what you stand for, or you can take control by using social media as your own personal billboard.

Remember, also, that you reflect not just yourself on social media but your team, your family, your town, and your school or organization.

The wonderful thing about social media is the opportunity it provides to engage with fans. Answering questions, retweeting or simply mentioning fans by name can be as significant as signing an autograph. On the flip side, as you probably already know, social media is a magnet for trolls. Don't get sucked into responding to negative comments. The troll has nothing to lose by being a jerk. You do. Ignore them.

Today's technology allows anyone to take a photo or video at any time. Do you really want to pose beside a pyramid of 116 empty beer cans? No matter how innocent the circumstances— maybe you didn't drink a single beer—photos can create an image that can take years to correct.

You will be called upon to do interviews. Call the reporter by name (and ask for his or her name if you haven't been introduced). Look them in the eyes. Smile. Don't chew gum. Focus solely on the interview, which means putting away your phone and iPad. Body language and tone of voice have a greater impact on how people perceive you than what you say.

Having said that, your answers still matter. Anticipate what a reporter might ask: Did you hit the game-winning home run? Did you drop the baton in the relay? Did a teammate get suspended for punching a referee? Take a moment to think about what you'll say.

You don't have to answer *every* question, particularly if it is controversial—e.g., the teammate's suspension, a political issue. You can say, "I don't know much about it," or "What I'm focused on now is getting ready for the next game. . . . " or "That's not up to me to decide."

If a question isn't clear, feel free to say so—"I'm not sure I understand what you're asking"—so they can rephrase it or explain what they're looking for.

If you're being interviewed after a big victory, allow yourself to be excited and happy about it. Don't try to be cool.

One rule of thumb for interviews: Own mistakes, share triumphs. This means you take sole responsibility for dropping the fly ball in the bottom of the ninth—even if you dropped it because your teammate got in your way. It means sharing the glory of your game-winning shot at the buzzer, mentioning the teammate who passed you the ball and the coach who diagrammed the play. This shows integrity and selflessness.

Just as honing your athletic skills takes practice, so does honing your media skills. Think of every social-media post and every encounter with the press and with fans as an opportunity to shape your public image. The smartest public figures understand that good reputations don't happen by chance. They're built, carefully and strategically, one interaction at a time.

Snapshot: Social media is part of today's world. Apply a strategy to it, just as you do (or should do) for everything else. Identify three key qualities you want to project. If what you're about to post doesn't project one of them, don't send it out to the world. Once poured, water never returns to the cup.

SPORTS NUTRITION

Nutrition is so important. It can't be stressed enough.

—DWAYNE "THE ROCK" JOHNSON

Jordan Mazur is a registered dietitian (RD) and the coordinator of nutrition with the San Francisco 49ers. He is formerly the director of Sports Nutrition for Cal Athletics at the University of California, Berkeley. Jordan carries with him a wealth of experience working with athletes on how to optimize athletic performance through food. Jordan also has a background in clinical nutrition, working with clients of all ages in private, collegiate, and professional sports settings. In his current role, Jordan is responsible for overseeing the performance nutrition program for the San Francisco 49ers and provides the players with evidenced-based practice and education about sports nutrition.

Here's my Q & A with Jordan.

Q: What are some guidelines for proper meal planning (e.g., number of meals each day, number of hours between meals)? Pregame meal?

A: There is nothing more foundational, or functional, for any athlete than meeting their energy intake. What this means is ensuring that you are consuming the proper amount of calories per day according to your individual goals. To determine the number of calories that you need, it's most beneficial to visit with a registered dietitian who specializes in sports nutrition. Registered dietitians are trained and educated on how to properly conduct a full nutritional assessment of an individual, which gives them a deeper understanding of your current individual health and eating habits as well as learning more about your nutrition or body composition goals. With all of that information, an estimated caloric range can be determined.

Once you know this, you then need to start to plan your nutrient timing. This means how often and when exactly you should be consuming the proper fuel. In general, athletes need to eat smaller meals, more frequently than nonathletes. This means two or three larger meals filled in with two or three snacks throughout the day, for a total of five or six feedings per day. Why does timing matter? The human body is always in constant need of energy, or calories, to function properly (physical activity, metabolism, thinking, breathing, digesting, etc.).

Athletes often have different energy demands than nonathletes. For example, they need to balance school, training, conditioning, film, meetings, treatment—and all of that requires energy. By providing the body with the fuel and building blocks (carbohydrates, protein, and fats) to use as energy, we supply the body with a steady flow of energy to meet all of our energy demands of the day. Not eating often, or not eating the right number of calories, can result in declines in performance, mental fatigue, and low energy as well as potentially increasing your risk for illness and injury.

For example:

6:00 a.m.   Breakfast

9:00 a.m.   Snack

12:00 p.m.   Lunch

3:00 p.m.   Snack after school or before practice

6:00 p.m.   Dinner

8:00 p.m.   Evening Snack

When it comes to competition, the precompetition meal is key. This meal will give you the proper fuel for performance, and timing it correctly will allow you enough time to digest and store that fuel before game time. The pregame meal should be consumed 3 to 4 hours prior to competing, and be high in carbohydrates, moderate in protein and vegetables, and low in fat and fiber. And of course it needs to include hydration!

KEY POINTS
1. Meet your energy demands.
2. Eat consistently every 2 to 3 hours for 5 or 6 feedings per day as your schedule allows.
3. Pregame meal should be consumed 3 to 4 hours prior to start of competition.

Q: What do you recommend for snacks (e.g., types of food, serving size)?
A: Here are some great tips for making some golden choices for performance snacks:

1. Refuel every 2 to 3 hours to maintain energy levels.

2. Limit foods that are fried or in a cream sauce.

3. Sparingly use fats like butter, sour cream, and mayo.

4. Toppings can add flavor—like ketchup, light mayo, mustard, olive oil, light dressings.

Here are some great performance snack options to choose:

GRAB 'N' GO SNACKS

- Granola bar
- Protein bar
- Instant oatmeal
- Dried fruit
- Fresh fruit
- Vegetables (carrots, celery sticks, broccoli, snap peas)
- Hummus with carrots and celery sticks
- Peanut butter with fruit
- Whole-grain crackers
- Tuna
- Beef/turkey jerky
- Hummus and pretzel cup
- Greek yogurt with fruit or granola
- Cottage cheese with fruit
- Nuts and seeds
- Low-fat cheese sticks
- Pretzels

EASY-PREP SNACKS

- Hot oatmeal with mixed berries and raw nuts
- Toasted bagel with cream cheese, sliced cheese, or peanut butter
- Bagel, English muffin, pita as bread for a sandwich
- Fruit and natural nut butter

- Preportioned dried fruit-and-nut trail mix
- Whole-wheat English-muffin pizza made with tomato sauce and mozzarella cheese

Q: What are some good refueling suggestions post-workout or after games (i.e., right away and even next day)?

A: When it comes to recovery, you should think about the three R's: Refuel, Rehydrate, and Rest. The refueling part needs to include protein to rebuild and repair your damaged muscles and tissues, but it also needs to include carbohydrates. Carbohydrates are the fuel for high-intensity activity, or in other words, it's the fuel for your engine. You need to replace what you've lost during your exercise or competition. Depending on your size and intensity of activity completed, you want to aim for approximately 20 grams of protein and approximately 15 to 30 grams of carbohydrates for recovery. In general, here are some great refueling options.

Within 30 minutes post-game:

1. Chocolate milk and a banana

2. Greek yogurt with berries and granola

3. Pretzels with a cheese stick and almonds

4. Turkey sandwich with two slices whole wheat bread, 3 to 6 ounces deli turkey breast, and lettuce and tomato

5. Protein smoothie made with water or juice, whey protein powder, and fresh or frozen fruit

6. Muscle Milk or protein drink

ıre your thoughts about supplements for teen athletes?

.tes need to be wary of taking supplements. The supple-
ıdustry in the United States is not regulated by the USDA or
ınment agencies. During the teenage years, many athletes are
ʒinning to develop more and are looking to find that edge or
ɛcret potion to get bigger, better, and faster. The reality is, there is
no quick fix or shortcut. The best way to improve is through hard
work, consistency, and dedication.

When consuming a well-balanced and varied diet, supplementation is often not even necessary. However, there is a time and
place to supplement and if that's the case, then supplement smart.
Consult with a registered dietitian on what your goals are. Registered dietitians can help guide you to making the best decisions
when it comes to supplementation. First and foremost, the question
has be whether there is scientific research to support the benefits of
the supplement that you are taking.

If you do choose to supplement, then make sure you are taking
third-party tested supplements. Third-party testing organizations
test and review supplements for quality and purity. Two of the most
popular and reliable organizations are NSF Certified for Sport and
Informed-Choice. Any supplement that is third-party tested will
indicate so on the bottle of that supplement with the designated logo.
Although this isn't 100 percent guaranteed, it does give you peace of
mind that what is labeled on the bottle is actually in that bottle.
Without third-party testing, you have no way of knowing exactly
what is in that supplement. The supplement industry is so unregu-
lated that a supplement costing $80 and claiming to increase muscle
mass may actually contain only rice flour, sugar, or even sawdust.

KEY POINTS

1. Supplements are not needed if you have a well-balanced and varied diet.

2. A dietary supplement is "a product intended for ingestion that contains a dietary ingredient designed to supplement the diet," such as whey protein, protein/energy bars, creatine, multivitamins, probiotics, and fish oils.

3. Dietary supplements are risky, as they may contain banned substances and are not regulated by the FDA. There is no guarantee of purity and safety.

4. If you do choose to supplement, look for products that are third-party tested (NSF Certified for Sport or Informed-Choice)

5. Consult a sports RD to decide if a supplement is right for you.

Q: What are some guidelines for staying hydrated? What are your thoughts about sports drinks (pros and cons)?

A: Proper hydration is one of the easiest and most important things that an athlete can do to affect performance and health almost immediately. First and foremost, the human body is approximately 60 to 65 percent water, and in athletes that number can be closer to approximately 70 percent, due to their higher percentage of lean body mass or muscle mass. Muscle contains more water than fat does, so by default athletes generally have higher body water than nonathletes or overweight individuals.

We lose water in the body through three main methods: sweat, voiding, and breathing. Our bodies can't create water, so all of that fluid has to be replaced. Especially during exercise, even a 2 percent decrease in body weight due to sweating can negatively impact performance and cause early fatigue. Proper hydration and fluid balance is important not just for exercise and performance, but also for optimal body functioning overall.

Some general tips and guidelines for staying hydrated:

1. Focus on fluids throughout the day, not just around workouts.

2. Always have a water bottle with you or handy.

3. Weigh yourself before and after exercise to know how much water to replace: Drink 16 to 24 ounces of water for every pound lost within 2 hours of finishing a workout.

4. Track hydration by checking urine color—the lighter it is, the better you are hydrated.

Smart Hydrating

Sports drinks were originally created to help athletes with performance in hot environments where there is a lot of fluid and electrolytes lost via sweat. Over time, some of those sports drinks have become widely available for the consumer. Sports drinks are most effective in periods of high-intensity exercise greater than 60 minutes in length. In general, a sports drink is not needed for exercise that is less than 60 minutes, and water is sufficient. Sports beverages contain electrolytes (sodium, potassium, chloride) and carbohydrate (sugar) that are beneficial when used at the right time. Due to the higher concentration of sugar in sports drinks, stick to water, sparkling water, fruit-infused water, and sugar-free beverages around times that you aren't exercising, to avoid excessive caloric intake.

KEY POINTS

BEFORE EXERCISE

- Begin exercise well hydrated.
- Drink at least 24 to 32 ounces of water at least 4 hours prior to exercise.

DURING EXERCISE

- Drink water or a sports beverage every 15 to 20 mins:
  - 2 or 3 gulps of water if shorter than 60 mins
  - 2 or 3 gulps of a sports beverage if longer than 60 mins

AFTER EXERCISE

- Replace the fluids lost:
  - 16 to 24 ounces of fluid for every pound lost within 2 hours of finishing your workout

Q: What are some of the major nutritional challenges and mistakes you observe for incoming college student-athletes? How can they overcome these issues?

A: MYTH 1: I'M YOUNG AND I WORK OUT, SO I CAN EAT WHATEVER I WANT, INCLUDING FAST FOOD, BECAUSE I'M JUST GOING TO BURN IT OFF!

This is a common thing that I hear from many young athletes. There is the misconception because you are active you can eat unhealthy food. Eating to just eat is different from fueling your body as an athlete. Athletes are high-performing machines, just like a sports car, and so you have to put in the proper fuel and maintenance to optimize performance. You aren't going to put diesel fuel in a Ferrari. You also can't expect to drive a long distance with your tank on empty. Fast food is a quick fix or shortcut, but it does not supply the lasting energy you need to perform. Oftentimes, fast food is high in saturated or trans fats, sodium, and added sugars—most of which you will burn through quickly, leaving you hungry again shortly. Real, whole food nutrition will give you more bang for your buck in terms of nutrients, energy, and satiety!

MYTH 2: THE MORE PROTEIN THE BETTER, BECAUSE PROTEIN AUTOMATICALLY MEANS BIGGER MUSCLES!

Protein does not automatically mean bigger muscles. If that were the case, we would all sit around watching TV eating spoonfuls of protein powder and getting huge. A healthy regimen for building muscle is

1. Following a strength—training program that challenges muscles.

2. Adding 500 to 1,000 more calories each day to current dietary intake.

3. Eating foods that are both high in carbohydrates and proteins:
  • Grilled chicken sandwiches, peanut butter sandwiches, and Greek yogurt with granola

4. Eating several small meals that include about 20 to 40 grams each of protein, throughout the day.

5. Choosing lean animal sources of protein (i.e., dairy and meats) that are more efficiently absorbed by the body.

MYTH 3: EATING HEALTHY IS EXPENSIVE!

Another common misconception is the idea that eating healthy is expensive. The truth of the matter is, it may cost a little more, but you can still eat well on a budget. The trick is to plan ahead. Store-brand products are often cheaper and often contain the same nutrition value as popular name brands. Buying in bulk can help reduce costs—buying items with a long shelf life like rice, beans, and canned products will go a long way. Help your parents out by clipping coupons and making a list of the foods that you want them to buy and stock up the pantry!

MYTH 4: I CAN TAKE A SHORTCUT BY SUPPLEMENTING INSTEAD OF EATING THE RIGHT FOODS!

There are no shortcuts in life, and nutrition is included.

Supplements often advertise as a shortcut to hard work, but it is rarely true. Supplements only work well in conjunction with a well-balanced and varied diet. Spend your money on real food and nutrients before supplementing; your body will thank you. Plus, you won't run the risk of some of the dangers associated with supplements (page 152).

Q: Suggestions for making good nutritional choices at the school cafeteria?

A: Eating well in a school cafeteria can be a challenge, with so many options available, but remember, it is possible! We all have choices in life, but remember that fueling your body well will pay off in the long run, especially if you want to be athletically successful. Paying attention to your meals in school will put you at an advantage over other student athletes your age. Here are some tips to fuel with purpose at school:

- Eat a healthy breakfast every day. If you skip breakfast, you're more likely to eat unhealthy foods and snacks by the time lunch comes around.

- Get a piece of fruit with your meal. Aside from the health benefits, it will help to keep you fuller longer. Plus it can help to satisfy that sweet tooth of yours.

- Make sure to balance out your plate with some veggies. A fresh salad with a variety of ingredients is best. Don't ruin that healthy salad with your dressing choice—choose oil-based dressings instead of cream-based dressings, and drizzle in moderation.

- Drink water. You should aim to drink around eight glasses of water a day. Bring a water bottle to school and fill it at the fountain before lunch. It is a great way to get some of that hydration at lunchtime.

• Don't be stingy. Fueling as an athlete is not the same as eating less. It's not about eating *less*, it's about eating the *right* foods.

• Skip the pizza and nachos altogether and get a sandwich. Choose sides like whole-wheat pretzels, a baked potato, baked chips, yogurt, and string cheese.

• Wait on the dessert. If you get it, you'll eat it. But if you hold off on buying anything until you're done with your meal, you might decide that you don't want that dessert anyway.

• Skip the soda. Those little bubbles might fill you up, but go with water, sparkling water, milk, or 100 percent fruit juice.

• Don't try to be perfect. Everyone deserves a chili dog and fries now and then. Just be sure to balance it out with fruits, veggies, and a healthy dinner later on.

Snapshot: Food is fundamental to your health and high performance. You can't run a high-performance Ferrari on soft drinks. "Eat well"—you know what that means. Review the lists we've provided, which include yogurt, fruits, lean meats, carbs, and hydration. You'll be burning a lot of energy, but avoid junk food; choose quality food instead.

If you do this, you won't need supplements. However, if you decide to go with some supplements, after speaking with a registered dietician about your goals, then make sure you choose those that have been third-party tested. Otherwise, you might pay $80 for flour and sugar.

Take your performance to the next level by improving your hydration. Muscles are thirsty and using them produces sweat, so you need to replenish body fluids. Sports drinks work well during high-energy activity, but generally go with plain water, fruit-infused water, or other simple fluids to keep yourself hydrated.

And last, just because the food comes from the school cafeteria doesn't mean it's best for a high-performance athlete. Choose the healthier options and eat like a pro!

FINISH LINE

So, there you have it—advice from some of the best athletic experts out there today. They're helping elite and professional athletes perform at their maximum, and they can help you too. Their advice covers several foundation areas, and if you pay attention to these areas, you'll be a better athlete.

The first area concerns your mind and soul. This includes staying positive, mitigating distractions, and building up teammates so that you build up yourself. Learn how to meditate, focus your mind, reach out for proper counseling and help when you need it, and understand that there are things within your control and things you can do nothing about.

Next, take time to sleep. Sleep is the body's time to build and rebuild muscle, clear toxins, and settle in neural patterns. If you deprive yourself of sufficient sleep in the name of working harder, then you're not working smarter. Set up daily presleep routines to wean yourself off the day's social-media blitz and technology frenzy. Power down.

Implement a strategy for your online social brand. You don't need to post everything, but everything you post lives forever on the Internet! As you look ahead to a time when you're a sports figure giving interviews or a college athlete looking for a scholarship, consider what you post now. Implement some guidelines for yourself. For example, identify three key traits you want to convey to your friends, family, and those around you. Post only those things that show these traits. Be your best, offline and online.

Above all, eat well. What's put in a box, processed, fried, and fizzed is not premium gasoline. While your training and age will help you to burn a lot of calories, don't waste your precious high-octane engine on burning sludge. Drink plenty of water often. Remember to refuel, rehydrate, and rest—the three R's of successful athletics.

CHAPTER SEVEN

YOUR GOLD-MEDAL GAME PLAN

Stay hungry, remain humble and get better today.
—PETE CARROLL

ow can you pull everything together into a workable plan? *Plan A* is your primary objective, which involves establishing a mental plan of attack that gets you moving forward. Begin by checking your mental state against the *Mental Game Scorecard* (page 162). This will help you develop a winning mental practice and a competition *Plan A* (and maybe *Plan B,* etc.).

Next, create a preperformance readiness routine (i.e., warm-up) so that you are at full power when the game clock starts. Learn how to give yourself a winning pregame pep talk and make sure to watch for the typical mental errors that athletes make at major events. Realize that you are growing and developing the ability to have an emotionally balanced life. As you know early on, life comes at you continually with situations that create imbalance, ambiguity, and uncertainty. Therefore, it is vitally important to learn how to deal with this and to manage and control what you can, which usually means getting the best out of yourself!

MENTAL GAME SCORECARD

Without proper self-evaluation, failure is inevitable.

—JOHN WOODEN

Score your *Mental Game Scorecard*. In what parts of the mental game do you do extremely well? What comes less naturally? Be honest in your assessment. If you score high in everything, then you're already a gold medalist. But before stepping onto any podium, real or imagined, rate your current mental game performance to identify your strengths and target areas for growth. Second, think through what you need to do. What do you have to work on to develop your mental skills and strategies, to take them to their highest level? Third, decide precisely how you are going to use your mental skills and strategies both in practice and in competition. Fourth, establish your personal mental game plan and solidify your thinking so you'll be ready to use the plan when you need it. This is not easy, and it's going to take a lot of work and effort.

A working *Mental Game Scorecard* is provided here so that you can use it to quickly measure the mental state of your game. Put aside the cell phone and other distractions and take a few minutes now to think carefully and review your performance in training and competition over the previous three months. Honestly rate your current mental abilities from 1 to 10 (1 = low, 10 = high) for the following mental skills:

_____ **Enjoyment: I incorporate fun, play, and humor into my game and avoid becoming unnecessarily serious, dull, or uptight.**

_____ **Goal Setting: I have clear daily improvement goals and I know exactly what I want to accomplish in the long term.**

_____ **Mental Imagery: I vividly see and feel myself performing well.**

_____ **Self-Talk: I keep my thoughts simple, positive, and powerful.**

_____ **Confidence: I have a can-do attitude when I need it the most.**

_____ **Focus: I stay on target and in the moment.**

_____ **Breath Control: I breathe easily and deeply under pressure.**

_____ **Mental Toughness: I do what is hard and stay positive under adversity.**

_____ **Anxiety Management: My butterflies fly in formation.**

_____ **Body Language: I carry myself as a champion.**

_____ **Intensity: My energy level stays just right for the situation (not too up, not too down).**

_____ **Affirmations: I regularly repeat my power phrases with meaning and conviction.**

Mental Game Score: _____

How well did you score? The total score for the personal assessment can range from 12 to 120, with an average score of around 60. Build your mental game so that your total score is at least 84, or equal to a 7 or more for each item. Subsequently, strive to sharpen each skill. Keep in mind that these mental skills are interconnected, so working on one area of your mental game will also strengthen other areas.

Your mental practice plan. Here is an example of how your mental game improvement plan might look: Imagine that you scored lowest on "Confidence." It was scored accurately, so you can work on what needs attention. Do not just work on what is easy. Set a goal to emphasize that skill over 21 days, for example. Then, reread the section on "Confidence" in Chapter Two and review the seven questions while flexing your confidence muscle. Pledge to maintain confident body language and facial expressions as you practice. Identify a past peak performance and relive it in your mind. Keep track of this, either in a journal, on a calendar, or maybe the notepad on your cell phone.

Resolve to always be in the process of improving. That way you'll also be developing one or two of your mental skills during the day for a set number of days. You might do it for 7 days or for 21, but whatever goal you set—stick to it. Importantly, this practice does not have to be time intensive. For example, you can practice breath control (15-second breaths) when you're stopped at a red light, waiting in line, or during any brief downtime throughout your day. A "Go for the gold!" sticky note or dot can be a helpful prompt.

Your mental performance plan. Think of game day as "Showtime" instead of a time for practice. As Bill Shoemaker, a horse-racing champion, said, "When you're riding, only the race that you're riding in is important." In competition, this means you have to go with what you've got and it is not the time to be switching things around. Make whatever minor adjustments are necessary, but do not try to fix your game while playing it. Do not let what you *do not have* get in the way of *what you do have*. Recognize and maximize what is in you today. Stay in it to win it by focusing on what is working well in the present.

In terms of your mental game, set two or three goals for each competition and write them down. Identify specific keys to stay in a winning frame of mind for the full game. Write down your mental goals, or ABCs, by using the note function on your phone and take it with you to the competition. Serena Williams, likely the best woman tennis player in history, writes down reminders on a piece of paper that she keeps in her equipment bag. She looks at her notes during changeovers in a match. These goals should be worded positively and in the present tense so you can focus on what you want to have happen, not on what you hope to avoid (e.g., "Stay on target," not "Don't get distracted").

In selecting your mental goals for competition, determine the specific areas of your mental game that are most important for you to underscore in your game play at this particular time. Do you need to breathe deeply to keep physical tension to a minimum? Are you maintaining positive body language no matter what the competition is doing? Do you refocus quickly when distracted or after making a mistake?

The ultimate experience is to go out and battle to the absolute best of your abilities, and actualizing your mental game goals will help bring out your best in today's contests. Modify your mental game goals for each competition and decide what is most important to accentuate at that particular time and place. After a match, take a moment to reflect on how things went—all of the good, bad, and ugly.

Here is a sample mental game plan that you can use for competition:

My goal today is to engage to the best of my abilities. I will accomplish this goal by following my ABCs:

a. I play with purpose and passion.
b. I play one good play at a time.
c. I think, feel, and act confidently all the way through.

PREGAME MENTAL PREP

There's no substitute for consistency.

—DAVE GOODIN

Alabama coach Bear Bryant, one of the most decorated college football coaches ever, emphasized: "It's not the will to win, but the will to prepare to win; that makes the difference." Importantly, a preperformance routine is a detailed course of action followed regularly on game days so that you are mentally and physically ready to turn it on right when the action starts (rather than firing too soon or too late).

Put together your simple and dependable routine so you can get a head start over your competitors. Routines provide reassurance and predictability that can help to alleviate Pre-Competition Syndrome (PCS)—the added nervousness, excitement, and irritability most athletes experience prior to performing. If a match is important, you're going to get nervous. So know how to handle and leverage the situation.

A really good routine helps to merge the mind and body to operate as one unit on the field. A routine also provides a shield from all types of distractions, such as unsolicited advice from others or mind games (talking smack, etc.) from an opponent trying to psych you out. Learn to ignore such irrelevancies during pregame. For example, some athletes take refuge in their headphones by listening to their favorite music, whereas others close their eyes and visualize themselves executing their game plan.

Most of us have seen Michael Phelps wired up and seemingly *tuned out* on the pool deck just before a race. To the contrary, he's *tuning in* before getting on the block. He's totally immersed in his mental routine and uses the headphones to drown out everything else.

Here's a virtual coin to help you develop your own pregame strategy. The two sides symbolize how you thought, felt, and prepared prior to your *best* and *worst* games. What similarities and differences flipped the coin at these times? These contrasting performances (win or lose) were not coincidental or random events but were influenced by what you did *before* a competition. Maybe ask your teammates and coaches for their feedback. Ask yourself: What has worked well for me in the past? Do I need to lighten up with jokes and crank up tunes on my headphones?

What do you do before a game to set the right tone? Self-awareness is the key to setting up what works best for you:

• Do you listen to your favorite song(s)?

• Do you spend a few minutes visualizing optimum performance?

• Do you practice slow, deep breathing to quiet your mind and steady your body?

• Do you like to socialize with your teammates or do you stay in your own world?

• Do you avoid interacting with negative people to stay in a good mood?

Look for patterns in your mental and physical pregame tendencies to transform any poor patterns into top-notch patterns. What helps you to excel? What causes you to fall short? Go over various situations from past matches, both where you did well and when you failed. Try to find patterns or habits that may have occurred during three or more situations.

Consider how the environment affects us. What makes it easier to avoid distractions? Do you let the importance of the match affect the way they prepared beforehand? Are there any environmental triggers that set you off? Do you reach a point where things blow up? Has a teammate helped pull you back into the game? Has looking up to family and friends in the stands given you a boost?

Reflect on mid- and endgame patterns (e.g., Are you solid mid-match or do you experience a breakdown? Are you able to seal the deal to win the game?). Champions excel in clutch moments. That's why they consistently win. Usually the difference in winning and losing is only one or two baskets, or a mental lag here or there. When do you come in strong? Do you need to replicate that at some other point in the game?

After identifying your tendencies, formulate a plan of attack consisting of what you need to do mentally in order to achieve your performance. Having a working routine will help you get to the starting line with the ideal mind and mood. Sticking to your routine from one competition to the next will allow you to compete more steadily and reliably throughout the season.

In designing your readiness routine, especially for the hour or so before game time, determine how to activate your thoughts and emotions in order to fully tap your physical talents. Make sure to review your mental-game goal list the day before, and spend a couple minutes going over it during pregame. The same physical warm-up routine done in practice can also help set aside your mind from worrisome thoughts and help you avoid nitpicking your technical skills. Remember to focus on what is going well each day.

Remember to customize what works for you. A collegiate gymnast shared with me her discovery that dancing around and socializing with her teammates at meets helps her perform at a higher level in comparison to her previous custom of trying to spend quiet time by herself. There is no better feedback than seeing what works and what doesn't. Don't get trapped in a box if you're in a circle.

Unfortunately, due to stress, outside advice, or some unique new scenario, some athletes abandon their routine when needing it the most. Develop the discipline to stick to your routine before each and every competition, regardless of the importance of the game or your particular opponent. However, be prepared to adjust your routine accordingly in case there is a delay in the start time or you arrive later than expected to the venue. Make modifications when one component of your routine becomes stale or if you find something that better suits your needs. Give it a test run before a practice or training session to evaluate its effectiveness.

Important things to do after a competition include stretching, eating recovery foods, drinking adequate fluids, and appreciating and talking with others about what worked well in the game. Think only about the positives. This can be very important. Post-game exhaustion, a natural drop from a high, and various moments in the match that went your way or against are ripe for negativity. That negativity, however, is false or just an easier lower mental state. Think and talk positively to get through this period.

Wait until later in the evening or the following day—after your body has had a chance to rest and recover—to complete your game analysis in your *Champion Journal* or to reflect on what you could have done differently. It is important to review.

Do not get carried away by superstition. Most athletes have developed superstitions or keep lucky artifacts such as coins, bracelets, or clothing. Our beliefs about these personal artifacts can help us center ourselves and thus provide a great distraction from performance anxiety. Along with a good routine, artifacts can keep your good wolf a winner by serving as a positive prompt. These items and beliefs can help us in a situation, but don't forget that they are just items or beliefs; you are still performing and the game is in your hands.

American gymnast Danell Leyva is known for the "lucky towel" he has incorporated into his routine during competition. He was the 2011 US national gymnastics championships all-around gold medalist and went on to win the bronze medal in the all-around at the 2012 London Olympics. Like a tennis player between sets, Leyva drapes the towel over his head to keep out distractions.

At the same time, though, you should avoid becoming so carried away with props or rituals if they become distractions. It's cool to do a quick touchdown dance, but if the dance steps require you to practice for hours instead of practicing for the game, they're too much. If this happens, it could be due to anxiety run amok or some kind of compensating alternative. You will need to directly address the underlying causes of worry and stress. Superstitions and the like are, of course, not necessary for delivering great performances.

Tony Gwynn made 15 All-Star teams and won 8 batting titles during his Hall of Fame career with the San Diego Padres. He shared his stance on the topic of superstitions: "You don't work the way that I have worked for twenty years and worry about stepping on the foul lines." In short, keep your mind in the moment and in the game.

PERSONAL PEP TALK

Most of the time before I take the mat, I just tell myself, "Confidence," and, "You have this."

—SIMONE BILES

A quick pep talk to yourself can often help get your mind geared up before performing on the day of competition, especially when the Big Bad Wolf of doubt begins to howl. Pep talks should be tailored to your particular needs and competitive conditions. Here are five keys to an effective pregame personal pep talk:

1. Keep it simple, clear, and *powerful.*

2. Evoke previous success for confidence.

3. Tell yourself what you need to focus on to play your best.

4. Remember that there is nothing to lose and everything to win.

5. Make a decision to *enjoy* each moment.

Imagine for a second that you are a competitive track athlete. You are warming up on the track's grassy area, along with your main rivals. As you notice the other runners, the Big Bad Wolf of doubt begins to howl. In your mind, thoughts swirl about. That competitor from the other county looks really strong. Another runner beat you by two strides in a meet last year. Someone has come over and wished you good luck. But instead of feeling stronger, each competitor seems to be digging into your psyche. To manage this, here's a sample pep talk you could give yourself by using process or task-relevant thoughts:

> Okay, I'm getting all anxious; let's take a few deep breaths to clear my mind and get centered. I'm well prepared and ready to race. The other runners have to beat my best time. I don't have to beat them, I'm just running my personal best. Over and over again, I've visualized my start, mid-race breathing, and push for the finish line. It's time now to focus on what I will do to run fast and turn in today's best performance. I'm going to trust my mechanics, relax after an explosive start, and charge home on the finish stretch. I have nothing to lose and everything to gain. I'm going to cherish each moment as

it comes. I'm bringing everything I've got, so let's free it up! Have some fun, as I'm the Flash!

FOCUS ON CONTROLLABLES WHEN STRESSED

You can only handle what you can handle.

—ANONYMOUS

So much of what happens in competition is out of one's control. How you deal with this fact? Acceptance of what you can control is the key to ongoing excellence:

1. *Attitude:* Embrace the challenge of the moment

2. *Effort:* Do your best

3. *Positive self-talk:* Encourage yourself and teammates

4. *Body language:* Act like a champion

5. *Performance routines:* Stick to your plan

Focus on the things you *can* control, rather than on the things you *cannot.* On one side of the "focus coin," you can control your self-talk and the way you act, but you cannot control the flip side (everything beyond you). Which side of focus coin you choose is all that is within your control.

A self-reflection tip: What is one uncontrollable thing you need to leave on the bench when you step onto the field?

Each and every time you feel worried or stressed in competition, take two or three deep breaths, let go of the uncontrollable—past and future results—and get yourself back to competing right here, right now, one play.

MENTAL ERRORS AT MAJOR EVENTS

Be present, not perfect.

—JOE MADDON

Let's draw attention to the three big mental errors (MEs) athletes often make at major events or on the day of the big game, such as a playoff or championship contest. The big MEs are 1) overemphasizing the outcome, 2) trying too hard, and 3) tracking the negative.

Making these MEs leads to preventable performance slipups on the field. Champions win the game from within by putting a stop to these errors. Fortunately, there are mental corrections (MCs) to those errors that can be utilized. Regardless of what day it is, the particular opponent, or the game's significance, the top goal is always the same: Compete at your best from start to finish. Upon doing so, you will have achieved your best total performance on that day.

In fact, the bigger the perceived situation, the more you have to cut it down to life size. This is illustrated in the movie *Hoosiers,* in which a small-town Indiana high school is preparing to play the state championship game in Indianapolis. The players are overwhelmed by the atmosphere and size of the arena. In an imaginative fashion, the coach brings their attention to the physical dimensions of the court: The basket and court length are identical to their small home gym, reassuring the players they can handle the task at hand. The team can now channel its energy within the dimensions of the familiar court rather than worrying about the large crowd. The team can now trust the training and talent that helped them to reach this game. The team can now focus on playing the game and not on worrying about its magnitude.

Mental Error 1: Overemphasizing the outcome. Peak performance is available only in the present moment, so deciding to overemphasize the outcome of the big game is a costly ME and one frequently made by young athletes. Of course, this is natural because all the preparation has already been put into the effort, along with high hopes for winning (or reaching best times) or a fear of losing (or failing to reach best times). Making this ME by thinking too far in advance about the possible consequences of victory or defeat often leads to playing well below one's ability because the focus becomes diluted.

Minimize the magnitude of the big game beforehand. Don't think about hoisting the trophy; instead think about playing the game. If you are prone to overemphasizing the outcome when the spotlight is on, the MC you need to make is to *stop stressing yourself out about winning or losing.* If you focus on the process, the score will take care of itself. Execute your game or race plan step-by-step, thinking only of the next step. Don't let others lead you into talking about the outcome. People may ask, "What will you do if you win the division championship?" Or "You've lost to this team several times this season; what happens if you lose again?" As soon as you notice others taking you off course, or that you have wandered into thinking of what is going on beyond your team or worrying about the final outcome, make the MC.

Promptly redirect your focus back on your mission of mastering the here and now, making sure you are concentrating on doing your job. You can say something like, "My practice over the last several weeks has gone well and I'm looking forward to the game." Or "I know our opponent is strong, but we're psyched to get on the field." Work the process and keep it happening one good play (or shot or lap) at a time until the final whistle or you've crossed the finish line. There will always be an outcome, so no need to think much about it.

Don't allow your mental energy to be used up on thoughts about *what-ifs* or burn your pregame physical energy on external factors over which you have no direct control. This includes any irrelevant chatter related to the competition or the hoopla of the event. Remain centered on the purpose at hand from start to finish. Do this by paying attention to the little details or performance keys that are always within your control. This process orientation is particularly important when you are fatigued or the game clock is winding down. Don't chase the win; let the win find you.

Mental Error 2: Trying too hard. This is also a common ME made by athletes during a championship game, when playing on the national stage, or when going against a higher-ranked opponent. Due to the anticipation and expectation that naturally surrounds that contest, as well as mistakenly believing that they need to play better than their previous best, they become overeager to play.

Have you ever heard top athletes at a pregame press conference? They sound like the championship game is just another practice match: "We've played them earlier in the year and it was a tough match. We're ready to implement some of our changes made since then. We're going to focus on what has worked for us this latter part of the season."

Rather than trying too hard and becoming tense and reckless, play consistently through the whole game. There is a false belief that you must make a Herculean effort or have a superhuman performance because of the circumstances. There is the risk, however, of making this ME, which will deplete energy and only move players away from what's made them successful in the first place.

The MC you need to make is to *stick to what you know has made you successful*, including following your regular routine on the day of competition. You deserve to be here in this situation. If you are well prepared, you do not need to change anything else right before or during the game that you haven't already worked on in prior practice. Do your normal excellent job and battle to the best of your abilities—nothing else is needed. Trust the talent you have from training and be instinctive with your decision making and automatic with your physical skills. Stick to your game.

Mental Error 3: *Tracking the negative.* Demanding perfection in your performance (or insisting on ideal conditions) every time out is another frequent ME made by student-athletes. This is especially prevalent in major events such as the state championships. Many competitors do not stop and realize there is always some margin for error. There is a frequent misconception that every play, shot, or possession by you or your teammates must be perfect in order to win (or that your self-worth is at stake). However, making this ME will only move you from being up to becoming uptight.

The MC you need to make is to *follow the positive track* instead of tracking the negative. Put an immediate stop to any negative or Big Bad Wolf commentary running in your head after something unexpected or unwanted happens. This might be a turnover made by your team or a call missed by the officials. Refuse to get sucked into frustration, panic, or pessimism. Immediately leave the blunder behind (i.e., flush the mistake) or you will drag it into the next play or possession. There's a good reason for the expression, "Shake it off." You do not want negativity dragging you down in the next play.

When Plan A starts leaking, then plug it up with Plan B, even Plan C. Beyond that, just play. Always make a commitment prior to performing that you will do your best to take whatever happens out there in stride. Emotionally rebound and let go of the negative events or mishaps that will happen in the course of events on the day of competition. This champion attitude will help you stay cool and confident for the whole match and allow your talent to carry you forward. Last but certainly not least, never feel bad about yourself if you have done your best. Your value as a person is *never* on the line in your athletic endeavors.

SERVING IT UP AND PARALLEL UNIVERSES

Birds don't think about flying; they just fly.

—ANONYMOUS

Tennis is certainly not a game of perfect, and out-of-control things happen, like a ball hitting the net and dribbling over. The net is set at a standard height and it never moves up or down during the match, so all you have to do is get the ball over the net—easy, right?

Why then do many tennis players double fault on key points? They have hit good serves hundreds of thousands of times. The court and ball never change. They can probably hit the ball in with their eyes closed—but then double faults happen. This is because something changes, which isn't the ball, net, or court dimensions. It is *doubt* that cascades down from the mind to the whole body. Great servers, however, differ from others in their mind-set: The great ones see the ball going in before they attempt the serve. Sure, they might miss the exact mark they are aiming for, but it'll be close. The point is to see what you imagine and you'll have a better chance of realizing what you saw.

Imagine the following scenario on a Sunday at a future tennis US Open. Our hero, Debra, is playing tennis at the exact same time in three parallel universes. In each universe, she is up a set and serving for the second set and match in a tiebreaker at 6 to 5. If she hits her spot, she'll likely win the point and match.

- In the Bronze universe, she is too excited.
- In the Silver universe, she is too worried.
- In the Gold universe, she is calm and focused.

In the Bronze universe, Debra believes that winning this point will transform her life. Her mind fills with images of the spoils of victory. She is overexcited because she is anticipating victory rather than staying in the moment. Debra rushes through her pre-serve routine. She tightens her grip, tosses the ball a little too much to the side, and double-faults wide—a crushing outcome that puts her opponent back in the set.

In the Silver universe, Debra believes that losing this point will ruin her life. Her mind fills with images of disgrace and ridicule. She is trying not to miss rather than living in the now and being in it to win it. After stopping her pre-serve routine, and while nervously looking around, she tightens her grip, hits early, and double-faults into the net—an embarrassment.

In the Gold universe, Debra thinks, "Hit up, down the line, looking fine." She looks at the seams of the tennis ball and takes a deep breath. She's not worrying about making the serve, only how close she's going to hit her spot. All she is thinking about is staying loose on her serve toss and relaxing on the takeback. In this narrowly focused moment, Debra's only thought is *execution*. That is, she is concentrating on what she can do physically rather than the meaning of a make or miss. Her grip stays loose, she makes a fluid stroke, and she knows the ball is on the line and moving away from her opponent—a thrill.

Remember that thoughts determine feelings, and feelings influence performance. Debra's physical skills are the lone constant in all three universes. The excellence in the Gold universe reflects her right frame of mind, without the mental static about the meaning of the point that is disruptive in the Bronze and Silver universes. Her mind is clear (fogless) and her body is calm, totally centered on the task.

Debra accepts that making this serve would add to her life, not determine it—her self-worth and future happiness are not on the line. She is not troubled by what others would think about if this serve gives her the game or if she needs to hit another shot. With that champion's mind-set, she follows her serve routine and performs with total trust and freedom.

Always focus on the process and execution rather than worrying about the desired or—worse—the feared result, whether you are looking at making a clutch play to win a tournament or want to hit a personal best for the first time. Be Gold!

BEND, DON'T BREAK

If you can push through the hard days,
you can get through anything.

—GABRIELLE DOUGLAS

Being a teenager and an athlete is tough. As a teenager, you may feel pulled in many different directions: school, homework, sleep, health, jobs, friends, family, love life, and your many outside interests and activities, which might include hobbies, gaming, or the Internet. Being an athlete adds another important dimension to your life and you may find yourself struggling to balance all these different facets.

It's a good idea to think about how to create balance between your sport and your life. However, all of the talk in the media about achieving a total "life balance" can be misleading, because *everything* is constantly changing. In fact, the expectation that balance or perfection (or a manageable workload) is simultaneously possible in all areas of your life is a misperception. We are all just better or worse jugglers.

While one part of your game is on an upswing, another part may be on a downswing. Perhaps you are doing well in your sport, but you aren't spending time with your friends. Sometimes you feel 100 percent, and other times you feel ill. Occasionally you play well and your team still loses a close game. Sometimes the forces all align, and other times the universe sends a meteor at you.

There are also periods when a particular part of your life is your only focus, such as during training camp for football, preparing for final exams, or during playoff time in your sport. Demanding a total sport-life balance at these times is way too idealistic and most likely impossible.

Instead, stay centered by aspiring to find the emotional or inner balance in life's continuous imbalance, ambiguity, and uncertainty by flowing with changes and controlling what you can and accepting what you cannot. The celebrated 16th-century French essayist Michel de Montaigne remarked, "Not being able to govern events, I govern myself." Sometimes life deals you a very difficult hand. To perform at a champion's level, play the hand you're dealt the best you can—because that is all you can do.

The champion's mind-set is your ace. Learn it and use it. Ask yourself the following two questions:

1. How will I handle my current situation like a champion?

2. What will I do now to get to where I want to be in the future?

Follow Montaigne's advice and stop sweating the stuff you cannot control. Think like a champion and do your best to embrace the unknown future as it unfolds in the present. Manage and deal with the controllables by sticking to these reminders:

• Whatever is weighing on your mind right now, realize that this too shall pass.

• Focus your energy on problem solving in the present rather than worrying like crazy about the future.

• Take positive-action steps instead of succumbing to apathy and inactivity.

• Be assertive by supporting your rights and needs, such as taking the necessary time for your training and regeneration. Sometimes this requires placing your own interests above the interests of others. Learn when to say no to others and hold to it in order to reduce stress or stick to your priorities.

• Talk with friends and family or a specialist for help and support rather than becoming or staying isolated.

• Learn and apply self-care basics and relaxation techniques for tension release.

• Maintain a boundless sense of humor. Find the funny side or silver lining in your situation.

• Above all, take a goal-line stand in protecting the core values related to your long-term health, happiness, and close relationships. Success will come when these things are taken care of. As a thriving client of mine expressed, "Always keep your sanity over success."

FINISH LINE

Begin your well-trained disciplined action right here and right now to make solid and lasting changes in your mental game. You are fully equipped with the knowledge to build and implement a mental plan of attack that lets you move forward in the direction of your dream goals.

Now is the time to work on continuously honing each of your mental skills. Learn to make mental corrections when they matter most. When it comes to working hard and intelligently on your mental game, don't just talk about it, put your mind to it!

THINKING AND FEELING IS PREPARATION FOR PLAYING LIKE AN MVP

Find your passion and make it happen.
Be on a mission and live your life on purpose.

—GARY MACK

For many athletes, physical skills come naturally (or at least come early in life), but the graveyard of sports is littered with naturally gifted players (high draft picks, "can't miss" young stars—no names here, as everyone knows one or two or more) who didn't understand the trifecta: physical, mental, and emotional skills. Lack one and you might as well lack all three.

Contrary to what many believe, the order is mental skill (willpower) followed by emotional and physical skills—*in that order.* Everybody knows an underdog who became a big dog. How did that happen? Willpower over firepower. So the physically gifted, as well as the less gifted, should learn how to create an ideal mental state that matches their physical skill to perform at their best.

Remember, mind-set training provides an unquantifiable *competitive edge* (i.e., you know it when you feel it). As a young champion in the making, keep sharpening your mental skills. All your talent, all your training prepares your body, but how are you training your mind? Thinking about bad outcomes, worrying about letting down teammates, or feeling tense and tight? Every game should start with you putting on, like a glove, your proper mind-set.

Young champions know exactly *what* they are trying to accomplish (**Mission**), *how* they are going to accomplish it (**Vision**), and *love* of the challenge to make it happen (**Passion**).

M stands for Mission: What are you trying to accomplish? You are trying to do your absolute best to be *the best.* That's the objective, both as a *team* and as *individual* players.

V stands for Vision: How are you going to achieve your vision? By executing all the process steps outlined in this book, including a daily improvement plan and always bringing your best effort to the practice or game today.

P stands for Passion: Use your love of the game and the desire to compete as your primary motivation. Champions love the fight as much as the finish, the grind as much as the glory, and the journey as much as the destination.

This is your Triple Crown: know your mission, have the vision, and play with passion.

Memorize the following nine reminders for how you can believe in your mission (think big), maintain your vision (never settle), and keep the passion (stoke the fire), as this is the essence of mind-set training.

NINE INNINGS TO NEW BEGINNINGS

Regardless of the sport or a participant's level, the player's mental preparation helps them see the totality of their experience and thereby create a performance perspective to cherish, embrace, and dominate the moment. Instead of being *tight before the fight*, players have nine full innings of opportunities to become a champion:

1st Inning: Think gold and never settle for silver or bronze. Have the boldness to pursue what you want most in both sports and life. Make "think gold" your life's mantra and put it into daily action. Personal best is your ultimate victory.

2nd Inning: Accept yourself unconditionally. Sports are not a measure of your self-worth. Putting 100 percent of your time and energy into your sport does not equal 100 percent of your self-worth. Smart players, when not playing, do other things that contribute to their broader definition of self-worth.

3rd Inning: Move along the continuum from fragile to robust to antifragile. Seek out, respond to, and become stronger with challenges. Learn from triumph and disaster (treat them the same, hard though it will be) and commit to being better the next time out.

4th Inning: Recognize that competition is a privilege and a great opportunity. Two key words to use going into a game or a series are *privilege* and *opportunity*. It is a *privilege* to play on a team, and you should see it as an *opportunity* to show people what they can accomplish if they work hard for years (just as you did).

5th Inning: Know that you'll soon do what you love on the greatest stage. Savor big moments within the game's context. Whatever happens, it's still a game—so have fun. You've done the work, now enjoy the joy: This is what I love to do. I love my sport. I love to compete. I'm ready to go!

6th Inning: Reflect on how well prepared you are for the competition. Be the best you are NOW. The most you can be is the best you can be now. So envision your best, as you're already good or you'd be doing a nonsport something else. Smile while thinking, I know it's in me. I know what to do. Keyword: know (yes, of course you know).

7th Inning: Play in rhythm. Beat your own drum because that's all you can control. Find your own rhythm and follow it to the plate, starting line, penalty shot, or tee box. Keep it routinely simple, in other words: simplistically simple.

8th Inning: Feel the pressure and deflect it! Go after your opponent in fundamental and inspirational ways (rob a homer, make the tag at the plate, steal a base, or bunt in a run) and put the pressure on the other dugout. The list goes on in other sports: the dagger 3-pointer, timely steal, block from behind, thunder dunk, ice-cold free throws with less than a second on the clock, the ripped tee shot that blows past a fellow golfer's ball, the bombed putt from over two ridges, the one-hopper in the cup out of the sand trap, and following a great shot anywhere with a greater shot at the moment.

9th Inning: Own the moment in the moment. Let your opponent choke on the old bone of what if? No one know the game's outcome in the first inning or set or half or front nine, so lock onto your performance and execute with precision, while staying in the MOMENT.

Extra Innings? Mission + Vision + Passion (MVP) + FUN = The Young Champion's Mind!

ACKNOWLEDGMENTS

Many thanks to champion literary agent Helen Zimmermann for her outstanding guidance and support. The third time is the best yet.

Much appreciation to Mark Weinstein, my editor, for his direction and encouragement. I'd also like to thank Yeon Kim and Jason Wells and the rest of the world-class team at Rodale Books.

Special thanks to Christian Swann, Mike Mombrea, Cheri Mah, Joan Ryan, and Jordan Mazur for their excellent contributions.

My wonderful wife, Anne, and our darling daughter, Maria Paz, for their endless love and continuously cheering me on.

APPENDIX:
Q&A WITH DR. A

To further expand on the information presented in these pages, I have provided below my responses to several frequently asked questions from athletes, coaches, and parents.

Q1: What are the positive and healthy values in youth sports?
A: Pursuit of excellence, mastery, teamwork, fun, joy, physical health, mindfulness, commitment, work ethic, sportsmanship, maximum effort, great attitude, resilience, creativity, confidence, composure, humility, handling failure, patience, perseverance, goal

Q2: What are negative and unhealthy values in youth sports?
A: Winning as the only goal, winning at any cost, playing through injuries, over-identification as an athlete, fear of failure/success, guilt/shame, perfectionism, short-term success over long-term growth, selfishness, egotism, entitlement, and poor sports-life balance.

Q3: Why is attitude so important?
A: "Attitude is a little thing that makes a big difference," said Winston Churchill. Attitude affects our preparation, how we approach a situation, and how we follow up after something happens. A

negative attitude in any of these areas will take a person on a detour, while a positive attitude will keep them on a road of constant improvement, happiness, and success. How can you keep chasing being your best self if you have a negative attitude? Attitude can be developed and nurtured. This happens from observing others, receiving guidance, and practicing self-reflection.

Affirmations can help with attitude and focus. Another way to think of affirmation is ingraining a verbal pattern into your brain that triggers certain reactions, which point toward improved attitude and focus. The brain loves patterns, and it's easier to draw upon these patterns in the midst of competition. It is often difficult for people to write affirmations because we're not taught to do this. People in our culture are usually taught to compliment others and not themselves.

Q4: Why do you advise people to not be awed by the glitter of excellence?
A: Because there is also joy, growth, and success in grunt work. There's usually more grunt work than glitter in life, so we all might as well learn to appreciate it.

Q5: How important are goals?
A: Goals point your life in the direction you actually want to go. Goals are a marker, while happiness is unbounded. Keep in mind the difference. A person must learn to utilize the tools, methods, and approaches that work for them. This can be expressed privately or publicly, as long as goals are being met and preferably exceeded.

Big picture goals are great for motivation. Also, meaning and fulfilment usually are manifested when one has a larger view in mind—whatever that is. Progress does not happen in a straight line. Failure and slumps are inevitable. Therefore, it is important in life to learn how to deal with failure in order to get back on course again. Champions understand that it's just a process of recommitting to their goals and values. This might be more important than learning how to deal with success.

Q6: How can we achieve focus over the long term for as long as it takes to achieve our desired level of achievement?
A: This takes a plan, support, and milestones. It requires regular checks to make adjustments.

Q7: What do you mean when you say we should battle against our best, or gold self, and why is this so important to becoming a champion?
A: It is important to reach one's personal best, and external factors or competitors can provide some motivation, but one should ultimately strive for internal goals and internal motivation.

Q8: What do you mean by "train it and trust it"?
A: This phrase was coined by my colleague, Dr. Bob Rotella. It means there is no time to "practice" during a competition. At that point, one must let go and pursue the zone and flow. What emerges will, to a large extent, depend on what you have done in practice. If you've put in the time and focus in practice, then you must trust and let go in competition.

Q9: Can one succeed without talent?
A: To a large extent, yes, but only to a certain level. It's unlikely

that a five foot one-inch person will "succeed" in the NBA, as there are physical limits. Talent is just one sort of limitation and not the end all. The key is to get the maximum out of whatever talent we do have.

Q10: What are some of the hallmarks you have noticed in people who achieve greatness in their chosen field?
A: A common trait of champions in all areas of life is that they view everything as a challenge to meet rather than as a threat to avoid. They realize that it's all on themselves to get ready to perform, to get the job done, and to accurately self-evaluate to perform even better. Champions create their own success rather than playing the victim.

Q11: Vince Lombardi said, "The real glory is being knocked to your knees and then coming back. That's real glory. That's the essence of it." In your experience, is this how champions see it?
A: Yes. Many times one does not know how much is within until an unexpected challenge arises. When one can overcome this, the satisfaction is even greater.

Q12: How does one learn how to repeat successes?
A: Success builds, so start small and then add. Champions don't rest on their laurels. They keep setting new goals.

Q13: What is the difference between a contender and a champion?

A: A contender wants to just stay in the game, whereas a champion wants to win it all, no matter what. A champion usually has brought everything together through consistency in preparation, attitude, and performance that others do not achieve.

Q14: How is it possible to lose the game before you play it?
A: The body responds to the mind. If the mind is unprepared, the body will be unprepared. Many games are won or lost even before the first play. As Henry Ford said, "Whether you think you can or think you can't—you're right."

Q15: Is it important that we really want to win?
A: Growth, achievement, and happiness contribute to winning and ease the disappointment (never the acceptance) of a loss. Motivation does not guarantee success, but it improves the odds!

Q16: Is playing not to lose self-defeating?
A: "He who is not courageous enough to take risks will accomplish nothing in life," according to Muhammad Ali. Champions play to win!

Q17: When the pressure is on, does it make it more difficult to enjoy competing?
A: Pressure creates the zone, and you choose to be either in it or not. The great player is able to "slow" the game down as the pressure goes up. That player thrives on tight, crucial moments in all sports.

Q18: Should we compete with ourselves or only our competition?
A: Both. Ideally, though, the main competition is you versus yesterday. Each day is an opportunity to get one day better. It also depends on your skill level. If you are far superior to your competitors, then you will mainly compete with yourself. If your level is similar to that of your opponent, then you will definitely be competing against that opponent!

Q19: How can we develop self-belief?
A: Practice, competition, success, role models, support, informational resources, and learning from failures.

Q20: How can we avoid beating ourselves up over our disappointments and disasters?
A: Reflect on them and then dump them, forget them, put them in an imaginary bag and leave it at home when you go to compete.

Q21: Does gratitude play a part in success?
A: Champions have an attitude of gratitude rather than a sense of entitlement. Acknowledge the help and support of others and be grateful for it.

Q22: Explain the mantra, "If you wanna win, you gotta buy in."
A: Championship-caliber teams have a high level of role acceptance. These players embrace their assigned role (big or small), bring a positive attitude each day, and avoid behaviors detrimental to the team. Everyone buys into the team's mission and the vision

for accomplishing it. NBA Coach Lionel Hollins said, "That's what defines chemistry. Guys have roles; they respect those roles and play to their ability in those roles."

Q23: What are some of the habits of champions?
A: A winning mind-set and a daily routine, a willingness to practice more than others, a resilience during difficult times, an acceptance that much can be learned from both victory and defeat, and a simple love and eagerness to play their chosen game at least one more time.

Q24: What is meant by "Drop it or park it" regarding errors and other distractions?
A: Review mistakes during practice, but in a match situation stay in the zone and focus. Quickly acknowledge a mistake, then set it aside and stay in the present.

Q25: What do you mean by leaving your game behind?
A: When you leave the field, embrace and enjoy the nonsporting parts of your life.

Q26: Should you get certain types of people out of your life? If so, what types?
A: There's a saying, you can choose your friends, but you're stuck with family. As best as possible, bring people who support and inspire you closer and push those who are negative or destructive farther away.

Q27: How important is love of the game?

A: Why play at all? The more you love a game, the more the game will love you back. When one has the opportunity and/or privilege to enjoy a game, just remember that there are few other occupations that pay players to play.

Q28: Why is it important to always give your best?

A: We owe it to ourselves to be the best version of ourselves. Best not to show up at all if you are not going to give your best.

Q29: Must we learn to respond to defeat or is it all about winning?

A: Acknowledge each defeat briefly and learn whatever you can. Then focus on being the best that you can be.

Q30: What do you mean by "Release the brick"?

A: Ruminating about our mistakes and failures is like holding on to a brick. After a while, the brick is bringing you down. In response, release the brick, which indicates that you have learned from what happened and just let it all go. Practice a letting-go ritual.

Q31: What are the dangers of panic and what can be done about it?

A: Panic is natural and can be ignored after a few deep breaths. In a sport situation, the pros turn panic into passion.

Q32: What do you think about perfectionism?

A: By definition, no one will ever achieve it. All that remains is the journey through imperfection.

Q33: Can we control distractions?

A: No, as most distractions come from external sources. What one practices, however, is getting better at managing how distractions affect the mind. So practice good eye control: Look away from anything distracting you from the task at hand.

Q34: Apart from material rewards, what are the benefits in becoming the best that you can be?

A: Health, joy, and meaning in life.

REFERENCES AND
RECOMMENDED READING

Afremow, Jim. *The Champion's Comeback: How Great Athletes Recover, Reflect, and Reignite*. New York: Rodale, 2016.

Afremow, Jim. *The Champion's Mind: How Great Athletes Think, Train, and Thrive*. New York: Rodale, 2014.

Bandura, A. *Social Learning Theory*. Englewood Cliffs, NJ: Prentice Hall, 1977.

Brooks, A. J., and L. C. Lack. "A Brief Afternoon Nap Following Nocturnal Sleep Restriction: Which Nap Duration Is More Recuperative?" *Sleep*, 29 (2006): 831–40.

Clabby J. "Helping Depressed Adolescents: A Menu of Cognitive-Behavioral Techniques for Primary Care." *The Primary Care Companion to the Journal of Clinical Psychiatry*, 8 (2006): 131–41.

Csikszentmihalyi, M. *Finding Flow: The Psychology of Engagement with Everyday Life*. New York: Basic Books, 1979.

Davis, H., M. Liotti, E. T. Ngan, T. S. Woodward, J. X. Van Snellenberg, S. M. van Anders, A. Smith, and H. S. Mayberg. "fMRI BOLD Signal Changes in Elite Swimmers While Viewing Videos of Personal Failure." *Brain Imaging and Behavior*, 2 (2007): 84–93.

Dweck, Carol S. Mindset: *The New Psychology of Success*. New York: Random House, 2006.

Emmons, R. A., and M. E. McCullough. "Counting Blessings versus Burdens: Experimental Studies of Gratitude and Subjective Well-Being in Daily Life." *Journal of Personality and Social Psychology*, 84 (2003): 377–89.

Feltz, D. L., and D. M. Landers. "A Meta-Analysis of the Mental Practice Literature." *Journal of Sport Psychology*, 5 (1983): 25–57.

Green, Shawn, with Gordon McAlpine. *The Way of Baseball: Finding Stillness at 95 MPH*. New York: Simon and Schuster, 2011.

Hatzigeorgiadis, A., N. Zourbanos, E. Galanis, and Y. Theodorakis. "Self-Talk and Sports Performance: A Meta-Analysis." *Perspectives on Psychological Science*, 6 (2011): 348–56.

Jackson, S. "Athletes in Flow: A Qualitative Investigation of Flow in Elite Figure Skaters." *Journal of Applied Sport Psychology*, 4 (1992): 161–80.

Phelps, Michael, with Alan Abrahamson. *No Limits: The Will to Succeed*. New York: Free Press, 2008.

Ravizza, K. Qualities of the peak experience in sport. In J. M. Silva and R. S. Weinberg, eds. *Psychological Foundations of Sport* (pp. 452–62). Champaign, IL: Human Kinetics, 1984.

Rotella, Bob, with Bob Cullen. *Golf Is Not a Game of Perfect*. New York: Simon and Schuster, 1995.

Russell, Bill, with Taylor Branch. *Second Wind: The Memoirs of an Opinionated Man*. Random House, 1979.

Strack, F., L. L. Martin, and S. Stepper. "Inhibiting and Facilitating Conditions of the Human Smile: A Nonobtrusive Test of the Facial Feedback Hypothesis." *Journal of Personality and Social Psychology*, 54 (5) (1988): 768.

Swann, C., R. Keegan, L. Crust, and D. Piggott. "Psychological states underlying excellent performance in professional golfers: 'Letting it happen' vs. 'making it happen.'" *Psychology of Sport and Exercise*, 23 (2016): 101–13.

Swann, C., R. J. Keegan, D. Piggott, and L. Crust. "A Systematic Review of the Experience, Occurrence, and Controllability of Flow States in Elite Sport." *Psychology of Sport and Exercise*, 13(6) (2012): 807–19.

Taleb, N. N. *Antifragile: Things That Gain from Disorder*. New York: Random House, 2012.

Taylor, J. B. *My Stroke of Insight: A Brain Scientist's Personal Journey*. New York: Viking Adult, 2008.

Wooden, John, and Steve Jamison. *Wooden on Leadership: How to Create a Winning Organization*. New York: McGraw-Hill, 2005.

INDEX

P

Palmer, Arnold, 81
Panic, 52, 196
Participation trophy, 5, 11–12
Passion, 184
PCS, 166
People skills, developing, 17–19
Pep talk, personal, 170–72
Perfectionism, 197
Performance
    enhancing daily with
        reminders, 16
    establishing routines, 93
    feelings influencing, 51, 178
    imagining your optimal, 35
    increase with mental
        imagery, 35–36
    increase with positive
        thinking, 40
    keeping it simple, 93
    mental performance plan,
        164
    quality and intensity level,
        58–60
    report card, self, 4
    trophy-winning, 6
    winning mind-set and, 4
Performance anxiety, 52–55
Performance engine, 15
Personal responsibility, 139
Perspective, 79
Phelps, Michael, 1, 37, 45, 166
Popovich, Gregg, 31, 49
Posey, Buster, 2
Positivity, 39–43, 55, 62,
        140–41, 159, 169, 172,
        176
Potential, achieving your true, 5

Power down, 59–60
Power phrases, 61–62
Power up, 59
Practice
    breath control, 164
    champion's response to, 70,
        77–78
    competitive mind-set during,
        93
    focused, 90
    imagery, 102–3
    with intention, 54
    mental practice plan, 164
    "train it and trust it," 191
Pre-Competition Syndrome
    (PCS), 166
Pregame mental prep, 166–70
Preparation, 53
Presence in the moment, 46–47,
    186
Pressure
    deflecting, 186
    enjoyment of competition, 193
    managing perceived, 93
Priority management, 15
Privilege, competition as, 185
Problems, discussing, 18
Problem solving in the present,
    focus on, 181
Protein, 148, 151, 155–56
Psychology, sport, 96, 97

R

Ravizza, Ken, 97
Recovery, 14–15, 75
    refueling, 151
    sleep, 68–69, 142–44, 159

ABOUT THE AUTHOR

Dr. Jim Afremow is the peak performance coordinator for the San Francisco Giants baseball organization. A much sought-after mental game coach and licensed professional counselor, he is the author of *The Champion's Comeback: How Great Athletes Recover, Reflect, and Reignite* (Rodale, 2016) and *The Champion's Mind: How Great Athletes Think, Train, and Thrive* (Rodale, 2014).

Dr. Afremow is the founder of Good to Gold Medal, PLLC, a leading coaching and consulting practice. Though his practice is located in Phoenix, he provides individual and team mental training services across the globe to athletes, teams, and coaches in all sports, as well as to parents, business professionals, and all others engaged in highly demanding endeavors. He is passionate about helping others achieve peak performance and personal excellence, and reach their true potential.

For more than 15 years, Dr. Afremow has assisted numerous high-school, collegiate, recreational, and professional athletes. Major sports represented include MLB, NBA, WNBA, PGA Tour, LPGA Tour, NHL, and NFL. In addition, he has mentally trained several US and international Olympic competitors. He served as the staff mental coach for two international Olympic teams, the Greek Olympic softball team and India's Olympic field hockey team. From 2004 to 2013, he served as a senior staff member with Counseling Services and Sports Medicine at Arizona State University.

Dr. Afremow is a member of the Association for Applied Sport Psychology (AASP), the American Counseling Association (ACA), and the Arizona Psychoanalytic Society (APS). He has an

extensive history of professional activity, including conference presentations, corporate workshops, and publications in top journals and peer-reviewed publications, including the *Journal of Sport and Exercise Psychology* and *Olympic Coach* magazine. He has also served as an expert blogger on the mental side of athletics for *Psychology Today.*

Dr. Afremow resides in Phoenix, Arizona, with his wife, Anne, and their daughter, Maria Paz.